What Is
a *Waldorf*
Kindergarten?

What Is a Waldorf Kindergarten?

Compiled and Introduced by
Sharifa Oppenheimer

Edited by Joan Almon
Afterword by Cynthia K. Aldinger

SteinerBooks
2007

The articles in this collection originally appeared in various Waldorf kindergarten newsletters, published by the Waldorf Kindergarten Association of North America, Inc. (now called WECAN, Waldorf Early Childhood Association of North America). Introductions copyright 2007 by Sharifa Oppenheimer. Afterword copyright 2007 by Cynthia K. Aldinger.

Published by SteinerBooks
An imprint of Anthroposophic Press, Inc.
610 Main Street, Great Barrington, Massachusetts 01230
www.steinerbooks.org

The photographs in this book were generously donated by two Waldorf kindergartens: Garden City Waldorf School, New York, and Merriconeag Waldorf School, Maine. We gratefully acknowledge the photography as follows:

Daniel Hindes, teacher at the Garden City Waldorf School: cover, 6, 10, 14, 18, 23, 33, 34, 37, 39, 51, 53, 54, 58, 60, 61, 67, 69, 72, 73, 77, 83, 91, 100, 110.
David McLain, parent at the Merriconeag Waldorf School: 4, 13, 15, 16, 17, 19, 21, 24, 25, 27, 29, 31, 40, 43, 44, 46, 56, 59, 62, 65, 71, 75, 76, 78, 80, 84, 87, 89, 90, 93, 95, 98, 110

Library of Congress Cataloging-in-Publication Data is available.

Contents

Foreword

Joan Almon

WHEN I FIRST BEGAN WORKING with young children in Baltimore in the early 1970s my colleagues and I had never heard of Rudolf Steiner or Waldorf education. After a few months we were introduced to Waldorf ideas for the first time and quickly began to apply them. At first, they were just more ingredients in the eclectic soup pot we were creating. What astonished me was the response of the children. They seemed to enjoy everything we brought them, but they drank in the Waldorf offerings far more deeply than the rest.

We started by simply changing the rhythm of the day so it had a healthier breathing quality, telling fairy tales, and integrating watercolor for painting and tissue paper for collaging in place of denser art materials such as tempera paints and construction paper. The children seemed to breathe more lightly and happily, and I often had the feeling that they were like flowers deeply drinking in the sunlight. What was this, I wondered? What were they experiencing that spoke so deeply to them, even though we teachers barely understood it ourselves or knew what stood behind it.

Because of the children's responses I decided I had to go more deeply into Waldorf education and Anthroposophy, to understand what they were experiencing. Thirty years later I am still learning about what they were able to absorb so purely and immediately. Along the way I have come to love and appreciate the many wonderful elements that we work with in Waldorf early childhood education: the incredible power of creative play, both indoors and out; music, art, and the wonder of the word as presented in stories, songs, verses and conversations; and the deeply penetrating world of movement and of purposeful work.

I have been astonished by the young child's enormous capacity for learning through imitation, both through outer gesture and inner mood, and I've been deeply moved by seeing the fundamental laws of child development at work in children all around the world. Above all, there is the miracle represented in the unique genius of each individual child. Add to all of this the rich relations with parents and with colleagues, and a beautiful tapestry emerges that is greater than the sum of all the parts. Woven into this tapestry of Waldorf education is Anthroposophy, the philosophy and spiritual science developed by Rudolf Steiner. It offers nourishment to the education and keeps it alive and growing.

As a young teacher it all seemed like a miracle to me — that an education existed that recognized the essential spirit in every human being, including every child, and honored it. Later I began to take it for granted, as tends to happen with all things we become familiar with. But today I appreciate Waldorf education anew, for I see it as an antidote to what is happening now in early childhood education across the United States. As a nation we have lost our sense of the wonder of childhood, and of the importance of nurturing the creative forces in every child. Rather we create kindergartens and preschools that are highly academic and value children according to how many letters they recognize and how many words they can read and write. We hurry young children into what was once a first grade curriculum and then wonder why they are under such stress.

Maryland, where I did all of my Waldorf teaching, prides itself on developing academic kindergartens long before some other states conceived of them. Already in 1975 I visited a public kindergarten where the whole morning was devoted to academic subjects, often in a playful way, but never with any real play. That kindergarten seems mild in comparison to what is happening today, where kindergartens run all day and are full of academic subjects. In the county where I taught in a Waldorf kindergarten, public kindergartens are now full day programs and mandate a daily schedule for five-year-olds of 90 minutes for writing and reading, 60 minutes for mathematics, 30 minutes for science, 30 minutes for social studies, and one 25 minute recess. No time is allocated for child-initiated, indoor creative play, formerly a mainstay of the kindergarten.

In California they have even gone even further. There, many kindergarten children experience scripted teaching for two hours of their day, and are taught by a teacher who must strictly follow a script. It is so detailed that the teacher is even told which questions the children are likely to ask and how to answer them. Now this approach is also being used for four-year-olds in some California school districts.

Increasingly, the national goal in early education is to get children reading as early as possible, and long term consequences are of little concern. Indeed, there is no evidence of long-term gains from heavily academic preschools. There is, however, significant research showing serious long-term academic and social problems for children immersed in such programs, especially low income children. Yet such evidence is ignored, and the academic approach to kindergarten and preschool is taking hold like wildfire across the world.

What happens when young children's creative capacities are diverted into structured programs where everything is thought out in terms of specific goals and achievements? The creative zest for life dries up in children. Early childhood teachers now say that if they give their five-year-olds time to play they don't know what to do. They have no ideas of their own. In such circumstances it is not surprising that elementary teachers often remark on the burn-out they see in third and fourth graders.

And what happens when these children grow up? Young adults in their twenties are the first wave of children in this country who grew up without creative, open-ended play as a staple of childhood. I have heard from business people that they feel that as a group today's young college graduates are not as creative as earlier graduates were. A human resources director of a software firm recently shared that the young graduates they are hiring lack social skills. Her firm is spending large sums trying to help their young employees learn to work with others.

I now appreciate Waldorf kindergartens in a whole new way—as a sanctuary where the needs of young children for play and experiential learning are supported despite all odds. It is incredibly important that such examples of healthy, vibrant education exist as a counter-image to the prevailing norms in early education. Young children need to be protected, but not in the old sense of surrounding them with a moat and pulling up the drawbridge. I think the next great challenge for Waldorf kindergartens is to be open to the world, to share their insights and riches freely and to learn from the challenges and experiences of others.

We run the risk of thinking of Waldorf kindergarten education as something so delicate and precious that it must be kept wrapped in gossamer veils if it is to survive. Rather, I see it as an incredibly strong and vibrant education that thrives in very diverse, and sometime adverse, situations—in the townships of South Africa and the inner cities of the U.S., as well as in urban, suburban, and rural communities all across the world. The best protection for Waldorf kindergarten education is the ever-deepening commitment and on-going learning of teachers and parents. If that is happening one can feel confident that it will not only survive and grow, but also be of enormous service to others.

I. *An Overview of the Waldorf Kindergarten*

1. A Day in the Life of the Kindergarten

Research shows us that three essentials are necessary for the young child's learning: çrst, a broad palette of sensory experience; second, both vigorous and çne movement in response to sensory input; and third, the opportunity to imitate everything the child sees modeled in the environment. Each of these works in concert with the others to foster vigorous brain development. In the following article we are shown a living picture of each of these essentials at work in the daily life of the Waldorf kindergarten. These activities are the backbone of the academic foundation that parents look for in an early childhood program.

First, look at the sensory tapestry: baking, washing, sweeping, mending, singing, painting! Imagine the scent of bread baking, the warm sudsy water for washing, the muscle power of sweeping, the çne eye-hand coordination of mending and sewing. Imagine the visual education in the dancing watercolors. And if you have had the great pleasure of sitting in the midst of children's creative, imaginative play, you will know the happy sound at the heart of this beehive of activity. All this sensory richness is simply a day in the life of the children blessed with this remarkable education.

Now let's look at movement in response to this rich environment. Our çrst clue to the inherent movement is to notice how we language the structure of the day. We begin with baking time, then washing up, then sweeping, singing, and so forth. It is a language made of progressive verbs. The young child is a progressive verb, and the necessity of movement is honored and honed in the kindergarten morning. Perhaps the "pinnacle" of the day's movement is Circle Time. This subject, Circle

Time, is essential, and merits an in-depth look in a later article. Here, the children's movement is not free, as in the creative play time, or outdoor time, nor is it "instructed" as in a formal dance lesson. Rather it is "shaped" or "formed" by the joyful invitation of the teacher's own delight in movement. Here, through imitation, the children are led to gallop, tiptoe, tap, leap, rock, sway ... all through the medium of story, song, poetry, and music.

In this beautiful, living picture offered by Ingebord Schöttner, we can get a feel for the role of imitation and the central importance of the adult, who models for the child what it is to be human. Each kindergarten teacher will imbue the atmosphere of the room with her or his own unique essence. One teacher may fill the room with song and model an excellent use of language, another may feel more drawn to the realm of imagination, creating little stories throughout the day, which are then reflected in the children's imaginative play, while another may focus on work activities, sawing, and hammering. And yet each one works with these inspired principles.

All this beauty given to the children is "nutritional." Their senses are stimulated, and through free movement and imitation of the adult, the experience is digested. It then becomes their own, nourishing their growth toward freedom.

Sharifa Oppenheimer

"WHAT WE WISH TO ACHIEVE," said Rudolf Steiner in his *Foundations of Human Experience (Study of Man)*, "will only be fully attained when someday … parents will understand that the first years of education pose a special task for humankind today." To perceive this special task is our aim.

Let us look at the course of the normal day in the kindergarten as it divides up, between 8:00 a.m. and noon, into free play, rhythmical activity, snack, walk or outdoor play, and story time.

In the course of this day, the kindergarten teacher works as the center. What she thinks, feels, wills streams out to her children as they approach her. They will with all their wills! The Center, the teacher, gives form to this will activity, not by her demands, but by her very being. What takes place in her being streams out in her actions; the child sees her and wants to do that too. And therein lies the foundation of the education in the first seven years: example and imitation. What the kindergarten teacher does and how she does it works decisively in the development of the child.

The kindergarten is a big household. Parents cook, bake, wash, iron and mend, sweep and clean; and the same things happen here. Singing belongs with work. Water colors and wax crayons are ready for painting or coloring. Sewing baskets are in demand. For diligent craftspeople there is a workbench. Brightly colored cotton beckons to finger crochet, knotting and plaiting. The little weaving frames are gladly brought out. Pictures are laid out with brightly colored wool. Rakes and little hoes stand in the garden. And before festivals there is the joyous preparation of the room.

The day begins with free play. How is this free play time given shape and form? During this time, the teacher, for example, works deliberately and consciously so as to leave the children free. She works and she carries out the work carefully. Let us suppose, for example, that she sews. Children come into the room. They are attracted by the activity. They watch a moment.

Some immediately get needle and thread. One child runs out to a play corner, gets a cloth and sews with her finger. Another irons a cloth with a stick of wood, folds it in a special way, and, lo, it is sewn!

Other children have taken up extensive play of some kind. Some bounce around; and one sits, finger in mouth, and seems to dream away. One of the bouncers, when asked, brings the teacher a cloth that was lying on the floor. Suddenly she takes an interest in the sewing, sits down and goes to work. The others who were "playing" with her follow her. With no great fuss, the group gets into purposeful occupation. The finger sucker may find it hard to play even at home. It is often a long time before he can get into any activity; the patience of the teacher can help him.

During free play time all is in motion and an air of "you may" pervades the room. A healthy child naturally perceives the objects in the room as his property; they are tools for creation. A piece of wood becomes a doll, a disk cut from a tree limb becomes bread, a piece of wood carved to suggest a

house serves nonetheless well as a chimney with wool as smoke.

Cleaning up ends the free play time. It is important that the children and teacher clean up together. And cleaning up can also be play: a storekeeper sells cloths for cleaning; the trash collectors gather up what is lying around; mother and father put their house in order.

Some children are already sitting in a corner beginning to talk together. Gradually one can come to washing hands and combing hair.

Then a particular song and a rhyme lead over into the rhythmical part of the day. Now the teacher, for example, works consciously on forming the movements. Contraction, expansion, and again contraction—therein lies the rhythm. As with everything in the kindergarten, this part of the day is in tune with the season.

It is very valuable if the rhythmic part of the day can be built up in blocks lasting three or four weeks. Little plays based on fairy stories can, to the joy of the children, be carried through two or three months. Rhythmic repetition sets the tone for this part of the day. Conscious movements and careful articulation invigorate both speech and play.

A rhyme announces snack time. If the snack can be prepared in the kindergarten, the process will enrich the whole morning's activity. If that is not possible, then the teacher is grateful if the snack bag of a child contains something simple; a roll, an apple are sufficient.

After the snack, it is time to play in the yard or to go for a short walk. A stone along the way, a stick, the sand, a tree, a waving leaf, a blade of grass, perhaps a beetle, a snail, some insect, the blue sky, the clouds, the wind, the murmuring brook, or a bird—all these are experienced by the child in the way that the example, the teacher, perceives and experiences them.

Back in the room, a story concludes the morning. The pictorial speech of the fairy story is language education in the highest sense. The Word, used like gesture in an image created by speech, loosens up a one-sided way of forming concepts and enriches the fantasy. Folk tales are treasures of wisdom. Children can still directly experience the image of the tale, and its figures take on life before them.

If we look back on the course of the day in the kindergarten, we can say that the seed planted by the teacher can bear fruit only with the cooperation of the parents. So to the day of the kindergarten teacher belong visits with the parents, meditation and a looking back on the children as they were during the day—the after-work as well as the fore-work for the time with the children—and some artistic or cultural activity, work with herself and on herself.

To find the special task of the first years of life requires, above all, a conscious and loving devotion to the child.

Ingeborg Schöttner,
Germany, International Waldorf
Kindergarten Association

2. Handwork in the Kindergarten

In our highly technological society, with unimaginable conveniences one push of a button away, it has become difficult for us to understand the critical importance of a broad, balanced training of the hand. In his book *The Hand: How it Shapes the Brain, Language and Culture*,[1] neurologist Frank Wilson traces the pivotal place the human hand, with our amazing opposable thumb, has played in the evolution of the species. The density of nerve endings in the fingers is enormous, and when these are engaged by lively hand activities in childhood, neural pathways of learning are laid down in the brain that will serve the person in every pursuit of a lifetime, including those considered purely "academic."

For millennia, human hands have been engaged in shaping the realities of life. Every tribe, grouping, and culture has understood the necessity to train the young in this essential work. Think through the activities of a human life in any society until recent ones, and you will see a wide use of the capacities and dexterity of the hand. Until recently children were taught to plow, sow, weed, cultivate, graft, transplant, harvest, thresh, grind, bake. They were taught to dig the mud, form the clay, turn the wheel, center, shape the vase, to mix precisely the glaze, to fire the kiln, to sand and finish the fired pot. Hands learned to help the ewe with lambing, to tend and feed the lambs, to shepherd the flock, to shear the wool, to wash, card, dye, spin, weave, and knit. Earlier cultures, although lacking the privileges of the

modern world, passed on the essential privilege of a well-trained hand. I would like to see a book cataloging the essential hand activities that have engaged human beings since our earliest beginnings. It would be a lengthy book! Perhaps, through current brain research, we will begin to catalog the whole-brain activity, the way the different parts of the brain "talk" to each other, in the homely activities of the hand.

Through the training of the hand, not only is the whole body engaged, but the heart, and the mind as well. In the following article we see the delicate interweaving of the developing skill of the child's hand, the heartfelt relationship the child makes to her creations, and the wide imaginations of the mind this engenders. We glimpse, through these whimsical descriptions, the child's subtle work of creating an integrated self. A self that is grounded in sensory experience or a kind of body-knowing. A self that is in dynamic relationship to the world, through the shaping impact of the hand. And a self that can explore the realms of the mind with the engaged warmth of the heart.

We see, again in this article, the central role that is played by the child's imitation of the guiding adult. The adult begins to engage in the next step, instructional learning, at a later stage of development, in grade school. In these early years, it is essential that we allow the full range of imaginative possibilities to remain open. This open, flexible imagination will later grow into thought that is imbued with the unrestricted potential of the life force itself.

Sharifa Oppenheimer

1. Frank Wilson, *The Hand and How It Shapes the Brain, Language and Culture* (Pantheon Books, 1998).

Introducing unspoiled children of preschool age to their first primitive handwork is not difficult when one appeals to their imitative capacities and their love of movement. For the will to express itself in practical activities is a fundamental element of their lives. These first, initial works with their hands are different from the handwork lessons of the school in a basic way. In the school, there is a step-by-step building up of practice, learning and work. In the kindergarten there is a wondrous experimentation, imitation and new creativity—everything is still creative play. Activity and fantasy flare forth simultaneously.

The handwork in our kindergartens begins outdoors with the actual experiencing of nature. The garden offers an abundance of possibilities for activity, which appears in the life and play of the children throughout the whole year. The children are always there, wanting to form something with their hands out of blossoms and leaves, with pine needles and grasses, with bits of wood, fruit peels and seeds, with sand, stones, and earth. Yes, even in winter

they can model wonderfully with the snow. Just a few of these activities are briefly mentioned here. Through all their senses, the children grasp these seasonal activities from the world around them.

In spring, when the trees begin to bloom and the fir in the middle of the garden throws down its cones, there arises a game that speaks to all of the children, the wildest and also the most placid. We call it "decorating little trees." We search for a handful of fallen blossoms, flowers, grasses, pebbles. It is easy to place these ornaments in the somewhat opened fir cones, and even the little hands that are impatient and unskilled can do it; there soon blooms a little tree. Around these blooming trees, worlds arise. With further natural materials from the garden, pretty little things are tied together, wrapped round, placed within, braided and built. Thanks to the power of their fantasies, everything comes to life, going far beyond what is physically apparent to them through their senses.

An "art" that is especially appealing to the girls, is the fastening together of leaves. For this the leaves should not be too delicate or the needles of thin twigs too coarse. This work requires care and a fine sense in the finger tips. The joy is then great when the crown, the little hat, or the little basket holds together! And if it tears, one must just quickly gather anew and begin again. This belongs to the experiences of the five- and six-year-olds. One can recognize something of their temperament through this activity. Overall, one must stand by helpfully. One must be attentive and yet enter in as little as possible in order not to interrupt the stream of activity, thus helping along all the broommakers, switchmakers, grassbraiders, chivebundlers, wreathbraiders, and so forth.

In the fall, the colorful environment inspires additional lovely things to do. Here are just two examples of occupations of this season which awaken enthusiastic activity: When "grinding flour," the dry, crackling leaves are rubbed in the little fists and are added to water, bringing forth color as if through magic. Are there children who will not, with great enthusiasm, try to find out which colors can be produced by mixing water with leaves, blossoms, nutshells, or wild cherries? They will mix them in the water, stir it well and strain it out. They may laugh and dance with joy if they are allowed to dip snow white cloths of cotton into these colored waters. Even if their colors are pale, only a shade of brown, a tender green or a hint of yellow or red, this can be just the right thing, for later one can make little dolls of the cloths and their faces will come alive.

These diverse, loving occupations with objects from nature stimulate the preschool child's imagination and delight in creating. The child perceives, through a still-dreamy empathy, a multitude of forms, colors, and movements that are full of life. One should not overlook the nourishment that comes through the flow of reverence (and which is such a contrast to the stereotyped and unyielding play with Legos). These first experiences of basic human occupations such as searching, picking, wrapping, tying, knotting, sewing, dyeing, and also sowing, harvesting, grinding and baking come about through the child's own doing of them. Children grow into life through these first combinations of play and work. These occupations grow into real abilities in grade school where the children master the technique of knitting mittens or crocheting. Then a real knowledge can shine forth.

A pure and beautiful material that brings us to ever-new uses is plant-dyed sheep's wool. One can play and model with it in a way that is quite different from working with sand, clay or beeswax. A basket with colorful wool calls every child's little hand to reach into it and to stay for a while, playing with these fine, gauzy, transparent tufts.

An especially beloved beginning experience of creativity is the making of airy balls: each child may take one tuft. These can grow, when little fingers carefully pluck the wool, until it becomes a big, round, transparent cloud, swaying from one hand to the next. After this "snowy evening" or "thunder cloud" play is thoroughly enjoyed, we take the cloud between both hands and begin to round it, to turn it, to form it all around. Everybody will feel the warmth in the palms as slowly the cloud becomes smaller and firmer, until it becomes a little ball. In the hands it can be rolled and turned, going from one child to another, giving and taking, going back and forth.

Charming, never tiring games accompanied by songs and verses will capture the youngest children, whereas the older, more skilled ones will invent more dramatic games. For instance, from the flat hand the little ball is blown off and immediately caught by another child! If one puts the featherlight, round ball in the cup of the hand with fingers well bent and blows—then brrh!—it cannot get away anymore. It rolls and rolls, turns itself as long as the wind blows, rests for a moment and soon tries to run again. With joyful practice each one finds out that the little ball, breath and hand obey each other! It is easy to transform these little "turnovers." With the awakened formative force on the inside of the hand, the round thing can be formed into an egg shape. Through the slightest changes, the gesture changes. Small children are especially gifted at this.

If one now draws out the "small head" and twists the wool between the thumb and forefinger into a beak, a little bird will perch on the hand as in a nest. Although it is unfinished, or perhaps because of that, the child will be delighted and begin to converse with it. From fabric or tissue paper we can cut wings and sew them on the back with a few stitches. Finally the whole thing can be strung on a piece of yarn and tied to a twig so that it can be guided like a marionette from above. The child will run and jump with the bird. A rich play will develop from this simple wool, made from the abilities of the hands. Many more things can be created out of this little ball by modeling it further, sewing a few stitches to fix the form, wrapping it with spun wool or sewing on some fabric.

It is always interesting to see how well-rounded lambs will roll from one child's hand, while long, prowling foxes will come from another, and plump rabbits or lean dwarves from another. In the moment of the creation they will come alive, and with the joy of playing they will be placed in further scenes: the lambs belong with a shepherd, a dog and the pasture; the foxes will need their caves, the rabbits their hollow, and the dwarves their realm with Snow-White.

Children who are getting ready for first grade will develop a beginning story and will weave further with objects at hand: colored cloths, rocks, roots, or stumps will be brought together, and a little stage will be built on a table or in a corner. These little figures, which are able to come forth in the spur of the moment, become part of an everyday scene or fantasy-filled picture and bring about the very best of play. Frequently the younger ones are the grateful spectators. Open-mouthed, they live into what is in front of them, moving, speaking and revealing.

It can happen that the performers (the six- and seven-year-olds) are not satisfied anymore with using sheep wool tufts for shepherds or kings. Special figures in their proper clothes are devised. This calls for making small dolls. Some new hand skills can be experienced here, as well as learning to help each other. A wool ball as round as the full moon is placed on a rectangular cloth, certainly a self-dyed one, and skillfully put over the round head held in the small fist, while a neighbor ties it together with thread. Arms and legs can be knotted from the cloth that hangs down.

Children who have been busy all summer long with silky, velvety, rough leaves and flowers will now touch and examine the fabrics and make their choices; a shepherd needs a cloak different from a king's, and different not only in color. One cuts an approximate rectangle for these "doll clothes," and makes little folds around the neck; again a neighbor helps with tying a ribbon around it. A bunch of silk threads or sheep's wool is attached for hair with a few stitches and a knot, then eyes and mouth are drawn on—and there stands a little doll! These simplest little dolls, which only suggest the human shape, are usually loved wholeheartedly, because such a doll can do more things than the most beautiful and expensive dolls one can buy. It laughs, it cries, sleeps, leaps about, becomes ill, practically dies and then returns to school, and so forth. Why can it do all of this in flowing transitions? Because it is not perfect, only suggestive. The possibilities are open. Yes, something is created that must be continuously completed through the child's soul activities, which invent this or that and have to do it because no stiff, finished, forceful appearance of the doll immediately puts a lock on the activity of the child. These dolls need to have yet more outfits with crown and sword, shepherd's purse, hat and crook, apron, broom, umbrella, and even a bed and house, etc. During all of this activity one should never fall into creating the naturalistic or slip into criticism.

It is important that one uses beautiful, pure material to awaken the artistic senses and sensibilities. Moreover, it is important that an active adult inspires the creative forces of the children. Yet in the kindergarten, one should not work out of adult perfectionism. To do so will hinder a child who, out of sympathy and vigor, will try to imitate, but be clumsy. Only out of their own experiences will children acquire the right way of doing things. How ingenious and meaningful they often are!

Arising from life and from stories, many toys are made over the year, gifts of primitive workmanship that show the hand of their creators. Even without being very skillful with the materials, each child of this age is gifted to do everything in gestures and movements.

The task of the kindergarten today is to prevent the drying out of this seedlike lightness and smoothness in the limbs through too early an experience in useful, "unpoetical" handwork. The educational principles of example and imitation serve as key and path to an appropriate kindergarten education. The secret of leading a kindergarten class lies in letting the children imitate as many life circumstances as possible. Just as through imitation they learn how to walk, talk and think, so at the kindergarten age, the form of the life around them should inspire and shape the child's development. Everything that is artificial, devised, or systematically divided into learning steps will later produce a weakness in the life forces.

Dora Dolder,
Germany, International Waldorf
Kindergarten Association

3. Human Development through Art

As we saw in the last article, the education of the hand is the royal road toward healthy brain development, and therefore an integrated sense of self. In this article, we will look more carefully at the arts in general, as an education of the hand, heart, and mind, and at watercolor painting in particular.

Brain research shows us that movement is the critical underpinning of learning. It is easy to see that the arts, which engage the whole body, whether painting, clay modeling, working with çber, drawing, wood-working, sculpting or such, engage whole-brain activity, and therefore foster healthy, holistic development. The subtlety of the development of the heart forces, or the child's ability to relate to the self and to the world, may be more difçcult to see. Let's explore this question more closely.

Young children, who still experience themselves "at one" with the environment, move toward an artistic experience like painting with an unconscious "living into" the moment. Adults come to the painting experience differently, with the observing mind intact. We notice the large piece of damp paper, the small jars of color. "Only the primaries?" we might comment. We take in the whole arrangement, detail by detail. Young children, on the other hand, simply come whole, and give themselves wholly to the color. A brush of blue color across the paper and... for a moment ... the child **is** blue. Then a brush of red color, and an entirely new thing happens to their inmost being ... suddenly red! Their relationship with the world, the red or blue, is entirely a felt experience.

These feeling experiences begin to create parameters that, in time, take on the shape of a self. Thus, the self is formed in relation to the world, and the world is taken in through this budding of the self. This mutual shaping of the self and perception of the world takes place in the realm of the heart. As the child grows and develops, the arts continue to be a place in which the self can be explored and expressed in relation to the world.

In this article, we can see the power in the child's ability to make a relationship to the world of color. This understanding is beginning to be echoed in some recent healing modalities in which the power of color to shape and inform health is being explored. We also çnd, in this article, how the capacities a young child learns through imitation, while painting, metamorphose into will-imbued, heart-felt thought, one of life's most essential skills.

Sharifa Oppenheimer

Human speech surrounds the newborn child from the first day. It creates an atmosphere permeated with spirit into which children "breathe themselves." Children imitate, listen, absorb, and at the same time form themselves. Only through this can they become human and express their personal self through the word. Similarly, and in an equally important way, art—the highest expression of the soul-spirit forces of humankind—works on the developing child. In order for children to develop their human capacities, an "artistic environment" is needed from the very earliest days of their life. First, children take in their environment; then they work upon it themselves. Here it is especially important that the meeting with art which the educator offers is not only a gift, but also, at the same time, a calling forth of activity from the child. The cultivation of art awakens the hidden, creative, building activities and the soul-forces of the child. In this way each artistic activity calls forth a different perception through the senses.

In working with children of preschool age, it is necessary to create from the beginning an environment that takes into account the child's sensitivity to good artistic quality (colors, forms, wall decorations, sounds, toys, etc.) In this way a deeper effect is achieved with this age group than will be achieved through "art education" offered in a few spare hours.

It is clear that at this age practical activities need some specific methods. Even small children can find their way into a variety of artistic realms and work with them, but not with the purpose of getting specialized training. Certainly one does not want to begin preparing a child for a later profession such as musician, painter or sculptor. The possibilities for artistic activities for children include modeling with beeswax or clay, painting, movement games that carry a strong musical-rhythmic quality, and playing on simple string instruments such as children's harps or kanteles.

In the following paragraphs, the example of painting is presented. For the reasons given above, this is an experience that should not be viewed as leading to a finished form, but rather it should be assessed as an experience that leads to abilities that can be transformed throughout a child's life. But the most important point to consider in these efforts is the following: In this early stage children take in everything with their total being (as an entity of body, soul and spirit). What appears here in its embryonic form must appear at a later stage of development in one way or another. Along with this, one must realize that in the thinking or social realms, for example, there will appear capabilities, but also deficiencies, and their connection with the early artistic activities is not easily seen. There exists in human life in addition to the abilities that develop in a linear, step-by-step progression, those abilities that appear in various developmental stages in a whole new way through metamorphosis.

Watercolor Painting

MATERIALS: Wooden boards about 20"x14" (50:35 cm), painting paper, flat brushes about 1 inch (24 mm) wide, artists' watercolor paints, small jars for the diluted colors, water jars, sponges and small jars for stirring the paints.

The children particularly love to help prepare the painting table. They are always interested in observing every job of the grown-ups and like to be active by helping with such activities. First the tables are covered with an oil cloth; the water jars are filled and distributed. Next to every jar a sponge is laid, on which the wet brushes can be dabbed. The colors will be diluted in small jars and smoothly stirred, then poured into the color jars, and these are then placed on the table. The painting paper (absorbent paper, not too thin) is dipped in a water tub and carefully smoothed (well-fastened) onto a previously moistened paint board. Now the painting can begin.

Understandably, such a joint preparation with the children is only possible when the group has no more than 20-25 children. (In Waldorf kindergartens this is generally the rule.) It is especially helpful if one has not separated the children by age, but has rather combined them in mixed-age groups (from three to six years). Then the different abilities of the children can be well satisfied by the different activities of the watercolor process. While the three- and four-year-olds are fully satisfied when they can stir the colors and pour them into the glasses, the five- and six-year-olds take on more difficult tasks (for example, gathering together all the supplies that are needed for the preparation, cleaning the painting table, washing out and drying the glasses, and cleaning up). The children notice the repeated sequence of events each time the group paints.

The Painting Experience

Without a previous call to order on the part of the grown-ups, which would result in bringing consciousness to the activity, and without a presentation to the children or the introduction of a theme, the children dip their brush in the color, and its flowing trace is followed along the paper. The limits of the three primary colors—red, yellow and blue—open to the children a color scale filled with nuances of unbelievable riches, which they themselves can discover. Particularly for the four- and five-year-olds there is a joy of discovery connected with this process. For when the single colors flow together in various places and mix, there appear the "between colors" such as green, violet or brown.

Alongside the color play on the paper, which the children frequently experience with words of wonder or joy, there is also the changing color of the water in which the brush is well washed, which plays a great part in the painting. When the whole paper is painted and the colors glow and shine through the watery element, there enters into the child a moment of great satisfaction, which often flows over into the free play that follows the painting experience. The picture itself is no longer important to the child after it has been put on the rack to dry.

The five-and-a-half- and six-year-old children come to the experience differently. Already, before they dip the brush into the first color, they often have an image of a definite color that they wish to use or of an object such as a tree, a castle or a rainbow that they would like to paint. The combination of liquid color and damp paper does not allow one to paint solid outlines, which is all to the good for the further development of the fantasy forces. It often occurs that the children add a new color to the already started form, calling forth a new sense-association in their fantasy. While they are painting or when they are finished, these children will gladly tell the grown-ups or another child something about their picture—which color they especially like or what content they discover in the painted picture.

Even for the three-year-olds, painting in this manner is a joyful experience. It is most important that one does not expect them to master the individual techniques such as, for example, washing the brush before they place it in a new color. It is also not possible for them to guide the brush in a directed manner. Often they move their brushes enthusiastically or timidly back and forth on the paper, and one perceives that for them the movement and the trace of color is the most important aspect of painting. Mostly the three-year-olds are satisfied with one color, such as red, and they are only finished with painting when the glass of color is empty. When they get another color as well they do not add it by placing it next to the first color on the paper, but rather they paint over the first color. It is the same with a third color. The result is then a dark, undifferentiated surface, and the three glasses of color can no longer be distinguished one from the other regarding the color of their contents. If one begins with a single color and gradually increases the number of colors, then these children learn after a short time to paint laying one color next to another rather than painting over the colors.

The three-year-old children are mostly very quiet while painting and they are busily engaged with it, especially when they have their own paint jars to use. The four- and five-year-old children happily share with one another, in a more or less impulsive way, when something special develops on their paper. Among the five- and six-year-old children, the quiet, industrious mood again prevails and indeed in a thoughtful, careful manner. Occasionally while they are painting they will have exchanges with other children of their age regarding the colors or content of their paintings.

Learning to Paint Through Imitation

Preschool children best learn to paint as they learn every other skill—through imitation of the adult. Therefore it is most advantageous for the children to watch the parent, kindergarten teacher or older sibling paint. They grasp it in the way described as appropriate for their age if no instruction is connected with it. Either they want to paint right away while the adult is painting (the three-year-olds) or they want to paint by themselves at another time (the five- and six-year-olds). All of the technical tasks closely connected with painting, such as setting up and cleaning up the materials, will also become familiar through imitation of the adult. All the reservations about the amount of work involved are dissolved through the helpful activity of the children.

If the adult is careful to first wash the brush in the water jar and then wipe it on the sponge, each time before dipping it into a new color, then the child will follow this sequence more and more in the same way, for every healthy child has a strong inclination to go along with or imitate in fantasy play every deed or movement in the environment. Therefore, certain deeds of the adults work themselves much deeper into the young child than do words of explanation, which call for the child's understanding.

With the beginning of the grade school years, the free fantasy-filled approach to color is replaced by a more directed experience of painting led by the teacher's words, and usually in connection with what is occurring in the lessons of that time. The development of a painting then progresses through definite steps, and the results are viewed by everyone.

Metamorphosis in Later Stages of Life

In a conversation, when adults carefully bring forth their arguments, experiencing the different responses of their partners and at the same time allowing themselves to be influenced by these responses, then they owe this capacity in part to their experiences as young children with color and brush, which were their unconscious teachers.

What the adult knows as logic is always the inner result of a purposeful sequence of steps, which the small child takes in from the environment through imitation. The inner order in the sequence of the steps of painting insures a "useful" result. In adult thinking, the careful connection of individual steps leads to a sure conclusion.

One who at an early age has learned to pay attention to the strength or delicacy of color and to gradations in applying it, will later find it easier to apply the same soul capacities in social situations, for example in self-assertion and in acquiescence.

Painting includes processes such as being careful, paying attention, waiting, following the course of the work, experiencing the laws of color mixing, and applying color in varying strengths. All of these activities give ever-renewed stimulus to the gradually awakening soul of the children, helping them to grasp their physical body and make their sense organization and their limbs ever more responsive.

Naturally, children are not conscious of this. They do not reflect on what they are doing, but live intensively in the activities. In this way they have experiences at deep levels, which can wait there to be grasped consciously in later stages of life and to find expression in an ability to lead their own lives. These effects reveal the true human justification for artistic endeavors in the pre-school. Art is not just an aesthetic add-on to "real life"; as an exercise of continual striving, it can become the foundation of a truly human mastery of life.

Freya Jaffke,
Germany, International Waldorf
Kindergarten Association

4. Circle Time in the Kindergarten

The kindergarten teacher strives for the "Circle Time" to be a microcosm of the entire kindergarten day. And the young child's day in the Waldorf classroom is designed to be a microcosm of the great rhythms of life. Life's fundamentals are experienced during Circle Time: the slow progression of the seasons, the human response to this seasonal cycling, the variety and function of different rhythms and moods, the guiding force of music, the language of gesture, the power of spoken language, love as the foundation of discipline, and as we see addressed in each of the above articles, the essential nature of learning through imitation, and the essential role of the modeling adult.

Many different skills are shaped during the circle, all accomplished through this great gift of the child's ability to imitate. Here, we see the three essentials of learning—sensory input, responsive movement, and the imitation of the adult role model—woven together with grace and joy.

▲ The child's senses are delighted with song, music, the visual pleasure of each other's participation, the tactile satisfaction of clapping, tapping, wiggling.

▲ The child's natural imperative to respond through movement is encouraged through the different moods and tempos of movement introduced by the teacher.

▲ The child will imitate not only the words and gestures of the teacher, but will also imitate the teacher's inner mood!

In this article, Nancy Foster addresses discipline issues through the medium of joy! Yes, the teacher must study and prepare, memorize and work, but at the moment of Circle Time, joy is the foundation. Discipline shares the same root as the word disciple—one who follows out of love. Does the teacher love this

part of the work? The children will mirror this love back into their world, even into their own physical selves!

The child's motor skills are honed through the varied large and small gestures, and through the various rhythms that are introduced. Because this movement is led by the teacher, and is not "free," as movement is free during outdoor time or indoor creative play time, this can expand a child's natural movement tendencies. The child's language skills are enriched by the choice of poems, rhymes, finger games and songs. The young child's memory is of a different sort than adult memory. It is more sensory based, less conceptual. This body-based memory is strengthened by the way gesture is used as the underpinning of language. The gesture is begun just a fraction before the word; it is a lead-in to language. Because the circle is offered through a story line, the child's ability to create mental pictures is fostered. This inner picturing is essential to all future academic pursuits. Even the child's social skills are refined. It takes a clear sense of boundary to play these games with many little friends close by and not lose the thread or descend into silliness! This strengthens the sense of self-discipline as the child follows with love.

The circle is the pivot of the kindergarten morning. As the many aspects of the kindergarten morning flow naturally from one into the other, so too do the elements of the circle. Circle gathers the threads of all the aspects of the day and weaves them into a unified whole.

Sharifa Oppenheimer

RUDOLF STEINER TELLS US THAT TO STUDY A PLANT it needs to be seen in relation to the earth—Circle Time is in a way the same. You cannot look at it in isolation, but must see it in relation to the whole. We must look at the role of rhythm in the kindergarten as a healthy breathing in and out. The morning in the kindergarten can be seen as a landscape with mountains and valleys. But one doesn't want precipices! Nor should the landscape be flat. It must flow through all its transitions and this is to take place through imitation. We want the children to enter all of life through imitation, allowing the dream consciousness to continue. This doesn't mean dreaminess and floating but unselfconscious participation. When you are in the dream you're not analyzing it. The child is just acting with what is there. Imitation allows this dream consciousness without which they can't truly enter into what is happening.

We do not want to entertain the children for the morning, but we try to bring alive the activities of the home—taking care of the environment and all the activities involved with the life of the human being.

The circle is a microcosm of the life of the kindergarten, which in turn

is a microcosm of life. It should be a time of joy and serenity—serenity in the sense of underlying peace and security. Let us look at the circle in this context, including the needs of children of different ages, discipline, and festival circles. First, content: The ideal is that there should be a unity to the circle—one theme with one part flowing to the next. To begin with, one selects the theme. The most obvious is the course of the year. What is happening in outer nature with plants and animals and also what is the human being's relationship to nature through the seasons? What is the mood and what tasks are related to the different times of the year? Nowadays children do not come in contact with these archetypal pictures of humanity and life as much as they used to. Another aspect is understanding how the Christian festivals fit in with the seasons. This is a good way of bringing children into contact with life.

In planning your circle, you should include polarities of mood—gay and sad, humorous and sober, vigorous and gentle, etc. There also need to be po-

larities of movement—fast and slow, up and down, large and small, expansion and contraction, etc. These polarities bring a living dynamic to the circle, and also provide a possibility for variation later on as the circle becomes familiar to the children.

The presentation of the songs and verses can be done in a flowing way by saying little linking verses of two lines or so. These are best repeated to help the children catch up with them. This repetition is not so necessary once the children are familiar with them.

Repetition applies also to planning the circle. You may start with a given theme and add to it over several weeks. For instance during the Harvest, you may do the mowing for a few days and add the binding, etc. You do not have to start at the beginning each time—you may start part of the way through as the Circle Time becomes longer.

At Advent the material may be all new. Otherwise, one circle can gradually change to the next by bringing in one or two songs or verses in preparation. For older children, one doesn't want to do exactly the same thing day after day—the same theme but not the exact same combinations everyday.

Music—the "mood of the fifth"—is what we try to work with. It is not just that it is the mood of the fifth—one should also look for the musical quality. It should be dreamy and with a certain purity and simple good quality—beautiful and worthy. Folk melodies are often beautiful. Music in the mood of the fifth is not difficult for the children to sing, if the teacher is comfortable with it. This takes time and patience on the part of the teacher and it helps to know that this music is truly nourishing for the young child.

The role of rhythm is important. Before the grades, children are not usually able to walk or clap in rhythm, but we should have this rhythm. We must look at the tempo of our speaking and singing. The inner tempo of the child is quicker than that of the adult so we need to choose a tempo that is comfortable for them.

Children love finger plays, but do not do too many. Work with quality rather than quantity. It is sometimes good to use nursery rhymes and find your own gestures. One seeks imaginative use of words and appropriate gestures.

Traditional singing games are more common in the English and American tradition than in the German, and they have a role here, especially later on in the school year when the children are a bit older. They can be used when not doing a full and unified circle. For instance, for three days in the week one can do a full unified circle and then for one or two days one can do a circle with singing games and nursery rhymes or, if the unified circle is not too long, a singing game can be done afterwards. Some circle plays can be done with costumes, but we have found that Circle Time is better without costumes. Circle plays with costumes are done, such as the Nativity Play, the Three Kings Play or the Snow White Circle Play at story time.

The form of the circle: When done with young children, the circle often falls into the "bunch of grapes." This is fine for young ones. The older ones might correct a younger one but you don't need to expect it. When doing a singing game, holding hands helps to naturally form a circle. This form can be introduced gradually, and as appropriate for the age of a group of children.

The circle has significance with its roundness and unity and without having a beginning and end. This unity is good for the young child. It asks a lot of a young child to walk around the outside of the circle. Therefore it is often not done in the kindergarten, for it can create a sense of banishment.

Also we do not put just one child in the middle. If a circle game requires that someone be in the middle, the teacher first puts the assistant with one or two children there. Later she puts two or three children in the middle. If you want a farmer in the center, two or three children can be the farmer.

The role of the teacher is different during Circle Time than at other times of the morning. Free play moves at the child's tempo but at Circle Time it is the teacher who sets the tempo. She has the opportunity to bring harmony and healing. Her voice must be clear and pure with a light tone and not too low. Practice your singing patiently at home. Try to start circle on the correct tone—you can do this by playing "A" on the lyre before you begin. Hit the notes in a clear way, not sliding into them. Also, one should not use a "singer's voice" with vibrato, but a natural voice which can set the appropriate mood. Children are very sensitive to the tone of a voice.

Gesture is also very important. It is difficult for many grown-ups to form good gestures. We must make our gestures from the heart. Taking eurythmy classes is a real training for this. To find the right gesture, try to enter into the inner quality of the activity pictured in the verse. Eurythmy gestures arise out of the sound, word and tone. The kindergarten gesture finds its form out of the quality of the object or the activity of the object. For example, a eurythmist might form a gesture for "wave" out of the formative force sounding in the "W." A kindergarten teacher might form the gestures through imitating the flowing motion of waves. The resulting gestures may be similar, though their origin is different. It is a challenge to work with gesture; make smooth transitions from one to the next; don't use too many or too complicated gestures. The children can get silly if there are too many. Always work out of imitation and start the gesture slightly before speaking or singing. This helps the children to imitate.

The teacher has to watch what mood she brings to the circle. Be fully involved in each gesture, absorbed in what you're doing. Enjoy your circle and be well prepared and don't fly off! Be grounded. Prepare the whole thing at home, transitions as well. It helps to develop the gestures at the same time as you learn the song or verse. Keep preparing and don't have the circle become just a routine. Keep working with your material.

One can vary a circle play by making small changes or additions, such as "Let's go skipping to the wood" or "Let's all tiptoe to the wood." This keeps older children interested.

For candle time set aside a special time to acknowledge the spiritual as you do in life. There are different times that teachers have a candle in the kindergarten. Some prefer the beginning of Circle Time. A small season table with candle is moved to the center of the circle and a morning song is sung. The candle is lit and the morning verse is said. The same verse is spoken for the whole year and no gestures are used for this verse. The verse is followed by a seasonal song, after which the candle is snuffed, the candle table is removed, and Circle Time proceeds.

When doing the Nativity Play or the Three Kings Play at story time, Circle Time may be kept a bit more short and simple than usual.

Discipline. Everybody should come to the circle. "We all do it." You need to carry this inside you. There may be an exceptional child who really can't bear it at first. That's fine, they can watch quietly until they are ready to join. (This is rare but you have to be sensitive to it.)

We all join in joyfully. The basis for good discipline, or no discipline, is good content. Be flexible and try to plan an appropriate circle. Really work out of imitation. Don't say, "Now we're going to do this." Just start and don't

wait until they have all stood up or whatever. If you find discipline problems, look at yourself. Was I prepared? Did I enjoy the material? Was my voice too strained? Did I rush?, etc. The problem is often connected with the teaching. It could also be a particular child. Could one do something with the child at another time in the morning which could help?

Circle time should not be used as a time for "show and tell" or "discussion," as this will be too awakening and will disturb the children's mood. There are other times during the morning when it is appropriate for children to share events from home with their teachers or friends, and once this is established, the children can enter fully into the circle activities.

Nancy Foster,
USA, Acorn Hill Children's Center

5. Fairy Tales and the Image of the Human Being

One of our most human capacities is the ability, even the necessity, to make stories. It is through the use of stories that the developing soul of the child begins to know what it is to be human. For an infant, in the simple narration of the day, "Now we change your diaper......ah, that feels better. Now you're ready for a nap," she becomes aware of the unfolding rhythms of human life. For the toddler, stories of the simple activities in the home and backyard continue this shaping inéuence. When a loving adult tells stories to the young child about the robin family outside the kitchen window, she develops a particular picture of life on earth. This differs dramatically from the sense of life she forms when she hears, through the media, the morning news with stories of war and global warming.

The power of story in shaping human consciousness and destiny has always been well understood. Societies through all time have used story to inéuence and shape human behavior. It is through story that the results, consequences, and rewards of human choices have been shown. Story has also been used to remind humanity of the soul's journey on Earth. World wide, stories have recounted the human journey from our cosmic origins and have mapped the return path Home.

In the twenty-çrst century the power of story is still understood. Unfortunately, it is used by a legion of advertisers, who tell the story of a humanity that will çnd happiness only by buying the next product in a vast inçnite çeld of products. More hopefully, it is also used by the creators of a new future, one built on mutual respect for Earth, self, and others. But the most powerful hands that hold this tool of story are the hands of the parents and educators who touch the future through the hearts of their children.

In this article, we are shown how it is for children that fairy tales image not only the work and challenges of being human, but also the various qualities of soul necessary to meet these challenges. We see how it is through the natural process of identifying with the fairy-tale character, rather than through critical thought, which is a capacity that unfolds in adolescences, that children feel their way into the outcome of the story. It is through this heart attunement that they can navigate their way toward a more conscious choice of whom it is they will each become.

Sharifa Oppenheimer

THE FAIRY TALE ORIGINATES IN THE CHILDHOOD of humanity; it has its roots in another state of consciousness. It opens its treasure to the consciousness of today's adult only when he or she can appreciate that our manner of thinking has undergone metamorphosis and development, and that the history of humanity touches us most deeply when we understand it as a development and metamorphosis of consciousness. A dreamlike, experiential consciousness, which radiated feeling and was filled with images, preceded our scientifically critical, observant, awake consciousness, which is filled with ideas. Humankind's knowledge of the spiritual world, of creation, and of the meaning of the Earth, of fate and life's task were imprinted by the ancient mysteries on the imaginations of mythology and the inspirations of religious traditions. Thus, the truth of what lies behind the Sun, Moon, and stars, and in animals, plants, and stones, could still be told through imagination and human prayers. They also tell of what is revealed in the twisting paths of human life and in the struggle with all that is downgrading, violent or tempting, and of what, as the essence of humanity, steps from being unborn into existence and sees again its immortality in death.

Fairy tales are the remains of these mystery languages—and the children are passing through these stages of human consciousness. For this reason, they live with the fairy tale images and are warmed and fulfilled by them again and again. In the mysteries, one learned and practiced a direct spiritual view of the forces and models behind the senses. Out of this source of truth, from which the ancient cults of the world religions were also created, the fairy tale speaks to the unreflecting, experiential consciousness of the children; and the children create the formative forces in their inner humanity from this source. For that reason, Rudolf Steiner, who showed the modern, scientific consciousness the methods of exercise and meditation to gain anew the power of spiritual perception, speaks of fairy tales as healing to the soul of a child. Cosmic forces of structure and growth shape the child's body into its increasingly earthly and solid form. These same forces operate in the outer form of spiritual facts in the fairy tale images and nourish the child's healthy life forces. "The human soul has an inextinguishable need to have the substance of fairy tales flow through its veins, just as the body needs to have nourishing substances circulate through it" (Rudolf Steiner).

We can interpret fairy tales as answers to the ultimate questions about our outer and inner needs. Even for those of us who do not already experience the full meaning of the fairy tale with the sensitivity of the artistic person, it is possible to achieve a clearer comprehension. Preparatory work for this can be carried out. Modern people must earn their love for the child. Because the traditions of heartfelt relationships no longer exist, they must earn their inner comprehension of the whole of humankind in its childhood. Thus it is still worthwhile to create anew the fairy tale mood and the fairy tale reality.

"Poetry heals the wounds which the intellect hurts," says Novalis. With this, he means there is a deeper truth than that which the unspiritual, rational, scientific method has to offer. Every explanation for children of fairy-tale age, and even beyond, should be interwoven with this poetry. The sorry statements about cell division and chromosomes, which in their time must also be learned, express nothing of the truth about the preparation for human birth. Heredity, human love, and the spirit of the Ego seeking its fate are involved. Heaven and Earth have a share in it as well. Raphael filled the blue background, out of which the Sistine Madonna carries her child into his earthly life, with the faces of the unborn.

Whoever has been present at the moment when a small human body ventures forth, painfully, from the mother's body into the light of this world, knows the worrisome question: will the life of the soul, with its first breath and its first cry, move into this body not yet capable of life? And also knows the wonderful joy when, with the rhythm of breath, the soul moves in, and the birth is completed. The small lump of earth is loved and animated by God's breath—the picture of the biblical creation story reveals itself in its radiant truth: God blew the breath of life into Adam.

The desire for truth ought not to be an excuse to deliver explanations lacking the spiritual, especially concerning the riddle of humankind, which engages us with its own fate in the most moving way when a new, small person seriously changes the entire fate of a family or of a number of concerned people. The touching certainty of the child, that the human being is led to the Earth on the wings of spiritual messengers, ought not to be exchanged for the half-truths of a materialistic biology and the announcement of human beginnings from the physical body! The fairy tale of the stork is true. Its new interpretation in the material world, its sentimental or cynical mocking from the point of view of the "naked ape," has destroyed the power of its symbol.

We are grateful to the old revealing wisdom of the true fairy tale. It speaks figuratively of change, of enchantment, and solution and, again and again, of the secret of humanity. The spiritual origin of people, their tests, their changes, their victories and solutions are depicted. The child can sympathize prophetically with it right away. And all the "cruelty" that we see in the dance around the wolf drowned in the well is for the child nothing other than the blessed victory of good over bad. This victory confirms in children the trust with which they are so wonderfully equipped with in their first steps along the path of life. The fact that adults depict such pictures for them strengthens them to deal with the disappointments that the first encounters with the bad in this world and within themselves will cause. Thus do fairy tales also teach that the bad must be struggled against.

A healthy three- or four-year-old will listen to the fairy tale "Star Money" on a hundred evenings with an ever-increasing sympathy. There is no more penetrating proof than this, that the child experiences an imagination, a painting for the soul, in the fairy tale. It is only the intellect, not the feeling or will, that is ever finished with a matter in which it has once taken an interest. We stand before art, imagination, and religious truth ever-stirred anew; we are elevated, and the impulse of our will is strengthened to its best.

Each person needs a field of activity for his or her inner life, for willing, feeling, and finally also for the thinking soul. Children need this field of activity for the strength of their souls as do adults. If I do not present children with the images and the language of the fairy tales, then the contents of their souls will be supplied by idle talk. Car makes and money concerns, trivial, unimaginative bits of everyday conversation will rule the field of their souls, resulting in a field filled with weeds.

As the vocabulary of children grows, so does their capacity for experience. With the capacity for experience grows the joy in creativity, the inner kingdom. When children who are told fairy tales over and over again and then, perhaps, even act out the fairy acts themselves, they live and deal deeply with the vital fairy tale characters. Thus it happens that the "fairy tale children," in their first year of school, have a decisive advantage over their peers who have been cheated of the fairy tale world. They experience with greater differentiation; they experience more; they can express themselves more fully either in words or through art. They are open, can listen better, and display greater pleasure in creative endeavors. They form their thoughts into well-structured sentences containing unusual words from their vocabulary.

And what are the fairy tale films serving up? They are turning the imagination that blossoms from the lovingly spoken, descriptive words of the fairy tale mood into fixed, industrially manufactured pictures. They are shackeling and destroying the imagination. The fairy tale film breaks the sanctuary of the child and with the suggestive form of the picture's effect, it stamps stereotypes into the children's souls. Even adults who have seen a Fredericus-Rex film with Otto Gebuhr can sarcely rid themselves of this imprinted image and create, once again, a living, imaginative picture of the lonely Prussian king. A child who has seen "Snow White and the Seven Dwarfs" by Walt Disney is cheated of the ability to feel the real forces in nature and to experience

actively and creatively the spiritual reality in the world of the senses.

Children are not unfinished adults, but those whose state of consciousness allows them to be nearer to the spiritual reality than the adult is. "If you do not become like little children..." means there is no going backward. The child who is of the "Kingdom of Heaven," still lives unconscious and dreaming in its guardianship. The adult who is supposed to become like the child, and will possess the Kingdom of Heaven in the days to come, is the person who has achieved a knowledge of the spiritual world. In the language of the fairy tales, child and teacher have a language in common.

Helmut von Kügelgen,
Germany, International Waldorf
Kindergarten Association

6. Choosing Fairy Tales for Different Ages

Because the realm of story is so vast, it is a gift to have help distinguishing appropriate tales for specific ages. In this article, Joan Almon has given us guidelines to consider, relying also on the rudder of our own heart. Joan cautions us to be sensitive in categorizing such living stories as fairy tales. Let's keep this in mind as we read further.

The young three-year-olds will usually be happy with little nature stories, or stories that mirror their own day. The tone is lighthearted and cheerful. Teachers or parents can develop their own imaginative skills by trying out "homemade tales," stories made up on the spot, inspired by the activities of everyday life. While spooning out the child's oatmeal, one could tell a little story of the way grandmother made the best oatmeal in the world. Make it rich in sensory pictures!

Older three- and four-year-olds are ready for sequential tales, which feature a problem that is solved through patterns of repetition and order. Educators understand that sequencing is an underlying critical skill for all academic pursuits. The ability to read letters in sequence across the page from left to right depends upon a body-knowledge of sequencing. Tales like these, in which each action is built upon the previous action, all repeated rhythmically, lay the finest foundation for an innate sequencing ability. Later, for five-year-olds there are stories that tell the action from beginning to end, and then repeat the sequence backward to the beginning. Often these stories are told in verse. The magic formula of rhyme and repetition make memorization a natural outgrowth of imitation. Young children love to say the story along with the adult, and can remember every word! The young child's memory is grounded in the body-based knowledge of rhythmic repetition.

The four- and five-year-olds will love not only the sequential tales, but the beginning of what we would consider "fairy tales." Remember to choose stories that have a cheerful approach, a simple plot and resolution. Usually the story presents the main character with a problem, and then shows different human qualities and the results they bring.

When the children are five and six years old the story line can become more complex, following their more complex inner development. Now is the time that "good" and "evil" begin to appear. Remember that the young child does not necessarily choose good over evil through a conceptual grasp. Rather, they "feel their way" into the heart of the characters. For a while the selfish brother may seem to have ascendancy, and the child has an opportunity to vicariously sense the thrill of self-interest. But, when the story turns, and the compassionate younger

brother is given the entire kingdom, the child senses inwardly the gift of selfless-ness. The child does not choose conceptually, rather through the felt experience of the outcome.

Finally, when the children are school-age ready, tales of the little princess or prince, lost from the castle and wandering in the forest, become pertinent. At this age, children are beginning to lose a piece of their childhood innocence, their "at-one-ment" with the world. Now tales of more complex heroic journeys, with tasks that call forth various character traits, are needed. These stories create pictures for the child of how humans traverse the many passages we face in life.

The final choice, as Joan Almon reminds us, is always with the adult story-teller's own relationship with the story. Knowing this, we adults can begin the journey of developing a heartfelt connection with these essential tales of human existence.

Sharifa Oppenheimer

DECIDING WHICH FAIRY TALES are appropriate for which age group is a problem that faces every kindergarten teacher, as well as every parent who wants to offer fairy tales to children. Over the years, with the experience of actually telling the tales to children, one develops a "sense" for this, but in the beginning some guidelines may be of help.

Among the fairy tales, there are stories of varing degrees of complexity. At the simplest level there is the "Porridge Pot," while a considerably more complicated story is the beautiful French tale of "Perronik," the simpleton in quest of the Grail, who must overcome seven difficult obstacles. The latter is a tale for elementary-school children, perhaps just as they are leaving the world of fairy tales around the age of nine, while the former little tale is a delight to three-year-olds as their first fairy tale. They enjoy hearing of the little pot, so full of abundance, which overflows for lack of the right word. At this age, the children themselves have a sense of life's eternal abundance, which one child expressed to her mother in this way when told she did not have enough time to take her out to play: "But mother, I have lots of time. I'll give you some."

In almost every fairy tale, there is either a problem that must be solved, such as how to get the porridge pot to stop cooking, or a confrontation with evil, which can take many forms, such as the Queen in "Snow-White" or the various monsters that Perronik encounters. The milder the problem, the more appropriate the tale for younger children, and conversely, the greater the evil, the more appropriate the tale for older children.

Another aspect of fairy tales is that the hero or heroine must undergo certain trials or go on a complex journey before succeeding in his or her quest. In the original version of the "Three Little Pigs," the pig is nearly tricked three times before he is able to overcome the wolf. Three is the number that frequently arises in relationship to the challenges of a fairy tale. In this case, the tasks are not portrayed as very ominous, and the pig handles them with a good deal of humor, making it a tale well-loved by four-year-olds. In the "Seven Ravens," the daughter must first journey to the sun, the moon, and the stars in order to restore her brothers to human form. This is a tale that speaks well to five- and six-year-olds. An even more complex tale is the beautiful Norwegian tale entitled "East of the Sun and West of the Moon." Here, too, the heroine must go on a great journey to redeem her prince, and the journey takes her first to the homes of three wise women. She is then aided by each of the four winds. Yet even when the north wind blows her to the castle east of the Sun and west of the Moon, her work is not yet completed, and she is further tested before she is able to marry the prince. This is not a tale for the kindergarten, but rather one for the first grade or beyond, when children's own inner struggles grow more complex and when they are nourished by the more complex fairy tales.

With these thoughts in mind, I would like to divide some of the tales commonly told in Waldorf kindergartens into catagories of complexity. This is somewhat dangerous business, for the fairy tales are so alive that they do not rest comfortably in one catagory or another. In the end one makes decisions very much with a particular group of children or an individual child in mind. Please accept these divisions lightly, as mere indications, and take the time to develop your own judgments in this area. You may find it helpful to read a few stories from each category as a means of understanding the different levels of complexity.

1. The three-year-olds in the nursery or mixed-age kindergarten are very satisfied with little nature stories, or with a simple tale such as "Sweet Porridge." The older three-year-olds are often ready to hear the "sequential" tales such as the tale of "The Turnip." The turnip has grown so large that Grandfather cannot pull it out by himself, so one after another come Grandmother, grandchild, dog, cat, and, finally, mouse. All together they are then able to pull out the turnip. One finds many tales of this sort, which have a strong pattern of repetition and order. There are also traditional songs that fall into this category such as "I Had a Cat and the Cat Pleased Me" or "Had Gad Ya," a song sung during the Jewish holiday of Passover. Such sequential stories have the added advantage of being relatively easy for a beginning storyteller to learn. A collection of tales for this age group includes the following:

Sweet Porridge
Goldilocks and the Three Bears
The Turnip
The Mitten
The Gingerbread Man
The Johnny Cake

2. The next category of tales is slightly more complex, but the overall mood is usually cheerful and without too much sorrow or struggle. Four- and five-year-olds are usually quite comfortable with these tales.

The Three Billy Goats Gruff
Three Little Pigs
The Wolf and the Seven Kids
The Shoemaker and the Elves

3. In the next category come many of the tales that we normally associate with the term fairy tale and that we think of in relation to five- and six-year-olds. These tales contain more challenge and more detail. The main character often sets out in the world with a simple task to perform such as in the "Miller Boy and the Pussy Cat." Although obstacles are encountered, they do not weigh too heavily on the soul of the individual. Such tales include:

Star Money
The Frog Prince
Little Red Riding Hood
The Bremen Town Musicians
The Golden Goose
The Hut in the Forest
Queen Bee
The Seven Ravens
Snow-White and Rose-Red
Little Briar Rose
The Donkey
Rumpelstiltskin
Snow-White and the Seven Dwarves
Hansel and Gretel
Spindle, Shuttle and Needle

4. The final group that I include here are those fairy tales that are well suited for the six-year-olds who are making the transition to first grade. This is a time of stress for children as they lose their baby teeth and sense a departure from the heart of early childhood. (Fortunately, they still have a few more years before they make their final "fall" from Paradise.) Tales in which characters have a personal experience of suffering or sorrow meet this new phase of inner development in the children. Often these tales are not told in the kindergarten at all but are left for first grade.

Jorinda and Joringel
Brother and Sister
Cinderella
Rapunzel

A frequent problem that troubles kindergarten teachers is how to select tales for a mixed-age group. If there are three-year-olds present as well as six-year-olds, will the more advanced tales harm the little ones? My own experience, and that of other teachers, is that this is not a problem, provided the story is appropriate for some of the children in the group. This is an interesting phenomena, which seems to work as follows. In a mixed-age group with children from three to six, one can choose a tale for the five- and six-year-olds, and the three- and four-year-olds will be attentive. They may seem less focused than they are with a simpler tale, but they rarely grow restless. On the other hand, if one would tell the same complex tale to a group of only three- and four-year-olds, one would find that they do not attend to it very well and easily lose interest. It is as if there is no one in the group who can "carry" the story for the others. In a mixed-age group one can also create a balance in the tales by telling some that are appropriate for the younger children. The older children generally do not get bored with the simpler tales, for they are now old enough to see the humor in the sequential tales or simpler fairy tales, and they will laugh at the humorous parts while the little ones listen with full seriousness.

When choosing a fairy tale, another factor to take into account is whether a fairy tale is generally well known in the society, even if it is known in an different form. When a tale is well known, children often seem ready to hear it at a younger age than they might otherwise.

The final consideration, and probably the most important one, is the storyteller's own relationship to the story. Sometimes a storyteller loves a tale so much that the story may be told to children who are generally too young for it. It is as if the storyteller's love of the tale builds a bridge to it. When this love of fairy tales is coupled with an understanding of them on the part of the storyteller, doors are opened to the whole realm of life in which fairy tales are true and live forever. In the telling of fairy tales we too are nourished and brought back into this realm. Rudolf Steiner describes the fairy tales very beautifully when he says, "The sources from which flow genuine, true folk tales, which speak their magic throughout all centuries of human evolution, lie much deeper than one might imagine" (Lecture, February 6, 1913).

Joan Almon,
USA, Alliance for Childhood

7. The Seasons and Their Festivals

One of the hallmarks of Waldorf education is the celebration of the seasonal festivals. As we know, the Christian calendar, also, focuses on the cycle of the year. This is reflective of both Christianity's and Waldorf education's cradle: Europe's ancient agrarian base. In all pre-industrial cultures, religion draws correspondences between the inner human experience and outer physical realities. Human beings, therefore culture and religion, are deeply informed by the land, by the cycles of the Earth. But what is the relationship, this interwoven pattern between the celebra-

tion of seasonal festivals and the Christian calendar? For many years, Waldorf kindergarten teachers have taken this question into deep consideration.

In this article, Joan Almon helps the reader see into the depth of Christianity, to see the Christ being as a "presence which has never been limited to individuals of one religious persuasion or another. Waldorf education ... is not bound to one religion or another." It is true that Waldorf education is a spiritual education, recognizing and honoring the spirit of each child, teacher and parent, yet it is not limited to any one religious point of view.

The celebration of the festivals marks the cyclic relationship between "our lights" the Sun, Moon and stars, and "our darkness" the fertile Earth. In a way, the celebration of festivals can mark the conjunction of the two major vectors of physical reality, time and space. At a festival, we bring a third element, our timeless presence, a "moment outside of time" to honor the ground of physical reality: the dance between light and dark, as they sway to the rhythm of time's music. Perhaps we have had, or will have the opportunity to notice amidst the hub-bub of a beloved festival, the inner hush this awareness brings. It is what Evelyn Capel calls "the inner quality that can be apprehended only this once." This timeless presence can make the festival an "event of a lifetime."

In the celebration of a kindergarten festival, there are elements that will remain constant, year after year. These give a sense of the familiar to young children, offering them a sense of knowledge and security. The teacher will also weave other new elements into the festival to reflect the changing consciousness of the children, to celebrate their growth. A festival is not an occurrence that happens one day, and is then forgotten. There is a patterned "season" of the festival. Weeks in advance, the preparations begin in the classroom. Crafts may reflect the coming celebration, and food preparation can begin early. For example, for a harvest festival, the children might begin grinding wheat into flour with a hand-turned grinder. This can be carefully kept in a glass jar, as the children watch, day by day, the level of flour rising. Finally, the day before the festival, the children can participate in baking a festive harvest loaf of bread. Each year that a child attends the Early Childhood Program, the harvest loaf might be the constant element. But in succeeding years, the teacher might introduce more complex crafts, or tell a more advanced story to accompany the season.

As we have seen in all the articles above, it is the consciousness of the adult that sets the tone and models our humanity for the children. The celebration of the festivals challenges the parent and teacher to make conscious their own relationship to time and space in this particular, unique moment.

Sharifa Oppenheimer

A GROWING QUESTION IN WALDORF KINDERGARTENS and schools is to what extent is Waldorf education bound to the Christian religion and to what extent is it more universal. The answer points towards the modern mysteries, for Waldorf education is centered around the Christ as a Universal Being who has helped humans in their development from the beginning of time. Rudolf Steiner speaks of the Christ in the present time as dwelling in the etheric world surrounding the Earth through which each incarnating soul passes. His presence is felt more and more by sensitive souls upon the Earth, but it is a presence that has never been limited to individuals of one religious persuasion or another. Waldorf education strives to create a place in which the highest beings, including the Christ, can find their home, but it is not bound to one religion or another. The door is open for all to enter, and this openness can be reflected in the celebration of the year whose rhythm marks the changing relationship between heavenly light and earthly darkness.

In the Waldorf kindergarten we tend to live from season to season, from festival to festival, but it is also wonderful to reflect on the year as a whole. Rudolf Steiner's *Calendar of the Soul* is a means of sensitizing ourselves to the inner moods of the year and our soul responses to them. Working with the current verse and relating it to the verse for the opposite time of year is a step towards developing a consciousness for the year as a whole and for its powerful rhythms, which we experience inwardly as well as outwardly in nature.

When we look outwardly, we see the ever-changing face of nature as the Earth breathes in and out through the seasons. The farther away from the equator we live, the more full are the breaths, so that the contrast between winter's in-breath and summer's out-breath can be very great. As one picture of these extremes, the radio recently reported on a spot in northern Alaska which had, in mid-November, seen a glorious sunrise and shortly afterwards a beautiful sunset. For the next sixty-four days that part of the Earth would not see the Sun at all. Of course, in the summer they will have an abundance of sunlight, and all the growth of nature, which for most of us stretches over six or eight months, is compressed into two months of summer.

Being used to an array of seasons, it was hard for me to imagine life near the equator where the Sun rises and sets at the same time each day and where the temperatures fluctuate narrowly. Visiting Ecuador twice was eye-opening, for my Ecuadorian friends assured me they were very aware of the passing seasons, for although the changes were subtle, they were ever-present, and the rhythm of the year was of great importance to them. When I asked a Waldorf kindergarten teacher there how she would reflect these changes on the season

table, she said, through the fruits, for each month different fruits would ripen. This was one way in which the passing of time was marked, and I have heard a similar response from our colleagues in Hawaii, where seasonal changes are also subtle. In such surroundings one sees how strongly the human being longs to experience time as an annual rhythm, not only as a daily rhythm or a monthly rhythm. It is wonderful that nature provides us with rhythmic changes, both subtle and dramatic, to meet this need.

There is another aspect to experiencing the yearly rhythm. We usually think of the similarities from one year to the next as the seasons unfold. We take delight and even comfort in seeing certain flowers bloom in the same spot each year. But gradually we may also develop a sensitivity to the differences between nature's work from one year to another. No two springs are ever quite the same, in part because some are warmer or wetter than others, but one also senses subtler differences as we watch the seasons progress year after year. Evelyn Capel expresses this beautifully in the following passage, which inspires a new, subtler relationship to the seasons and how they may live in us and in the kindergarten.

"The background to the drama of human existence is the changing scenery of the earth's seasons. Winter changes to spring, spring to summer, summer to autumn in much the same way each year their magical transformations can be relied upon but the wonder of the magic never grows stale with repetition. Spring has come before, it will come again, but there is a particular note, a subtle effluence, a shade of feeling in this spring that has never been quite the same before and which will haunt the expectation of next spring, though it will not be realized again. A particular season can be lost to one's experience if, in the midst of the pleasure in finding again its well-known, often repeated character, the heart does not catch the inner quality that can only be apprehended this once. It is a joy to find in spring the crocuses coming into blossom under the same tree where they have been growing for years, to catch in the height of summer the familiar scent of new-mown hay, to catch in the autumn the blue smoke of a bonfire rising past the bronzed leaves still fast in the branches and to sense in winter that tang of a clear frosty morning. Yet there is, amidst the familiar joys, the thrill of the unrepeatable element that makes each season in its own year an event of a lifetime, if only one is awake enough not to miss it." (*The Christian Year*, pg. 9)

There are many books which have grown out of Anthroposophy and Waldorf education that speak of the festivals and that are helpful to parents and teachers who want to deepen their understanding or who are seeking practical activities to share with young children. Those by Rudolf Steiner include *The Festivals and Their Meaning*, a collection of lectures on the various festivals; *The Four Seasons and the Archangels; The Cycle of the Year*; and the lecture cycles on the Gospels and on Genesis. *The Christian Year* by Evelyn Capel also gives a clear picture of the cycle of the year in connection to the Christian festivals. Those seeking a deeper, more esoteric understanding will find Sergei Prokofieff's book, *The Cycle of the Year as a Path of Initiation*, very challenging and full of insight. Friedel Lenz's booklet, *Celebrating Festivals with Children* gives wonderful images of the Christian festivals in relationship to young children. For those seeking to understand the Jewish tradition, Rebecca Schacht's *Lights Along The Path* is a collection of stories that gives a fine background and commentary.

There are many practical guides to the yearly cycle and its festivals available from anthroposophic publishers. These include *Festivals, Family and Food; Festivals Together; The Children's Year; All Year Round;* and *Crafts Through the*

the Year. Other books of interest include *Earthways* by Carol Petrash, a collection of seasonal activities, and *Follow the Year* by Mala Powers, a collection of holiday stories for the family.

Most of these books and many others can be purchased from Steiner-Books. Please call 703-661-1594 to order books or request their annual Education Catalog for Parents, Teachers, and Children, or visit their web site, wwwsteinerbooks.org.

Joan Almon,
USA, Alliance for Childhood

II. *A Deeper Understanding of the Waldorf Kindergarten*
The Developing Child

1. Stages of Development in Early Childhood

We see in this article a masterful re-visioning of the question held by parents, educators, psychologists, and philosophers alike: Nature or Nurture, Inner or Outer? Here we see, in Freya Jaffke's work, the interwoven pattern of these forces according to Rudolf Steiner's developmental schemata.

We begin with an understanding that "three things must coincide if a birth is to happen." Two streams of energy from the parents join together, offering the inherited material from which the body is formed. The third necessary stream is a soul-spirit, a human individuality to "inform" this physical vehicle. The parents come together to offer the outer material needed, and the individual human spirit brings the inner force necessary to ensoul the body.

The parents offer the raw "clay," but it is the work of the child's human spirit to make this clay well formed, that it be useful for the needs of the soul's journey on Earth. We see a continuing interweaving of inner and outer, of nature and nurture. The human infant is born "unfinished." The senses must learn to gather and integrate information, the muscles and limbs must become choreographed and begin to work together. The vision must become differentiated, as all visual forms emerge from the pattern of the mother's face. It is the will forces of the human spirit, working outward into the materiality that bring this about. And yet, it is also the outer forces of the environment, working inward, that influence the integrative capacity of this spirit.

The impact of the environment penetrates inward and is digested by young children through their imitated behavior, their movement, and in the development

of their unçnished organs. They imitate all that they see modeled in the environment, and for young children imitation means movement, both physical and emotional. This movement impacts, and to a great extent determines, the formation
of the organs. For instance, if a child is offered the gentle sounds of nature and
the natural sounds of family life—human voices, the swish of a broom, the clatter
of shoes on the stairs—her ear will learn to "open into" the sense world. If on the
other hand, she is met with a barrage of household machines and the constant
background noise of the media, for protection the delicate ear will "close down" to
the sense world. This movement of opening into or closing away from affects not
only the ear, but the whole organism. This is true of all sense experience. We can
now see the effect of our highly technological society and the imbalance of "sense
education," in the many children with sensory integration problems. The capacity
of the human spirit to apprehend the world, to integrate it, and make it one's own,
is hampered by negative environmental factors.

Thus the tasks of the parent and teacher become evident. We are required to
work with the same elements that the young children themselves are working
with: the environment and our own inner human spirit. We must create a healthy

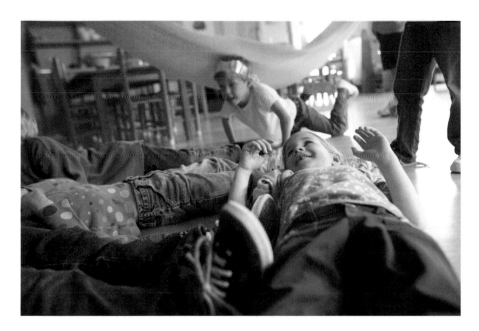

balanced "diet" of physical experience, for it is the work of the young to digest all that is offered to them. Digestion implies taking something in, for instance a carrot, absorbing it completely until the carrot exists no more, and its "carrotness" re-emerges as life force itself. The child digests all experience as completely as this, for the child has not yet developed the discernment to choose which experience to accept and which to avoid. This process of digestion is also called the miracle of imitation.

The child imitates not just the outer physical environment, but imitates also the inner environments of the caregiver's emotions and thoughts! We must be ever vigilant! We must strive to be a person worthy of imitation, for humanity can only be learned from human beings.

The three stages of development that the child's imitative capacity goes through in the first six or seven years mirror the regions of the brain. The early years focus on the nerve/sense system, thus developing the oldest part of the brain to function well in the sensory world. In the middle years we begin to see the functions of memory and fantasy emerge. These come forward from the middle brain, the limbic region. This is where "emotional IQ" is developed. Memory is based on "emotional flagging" of experience, and certainly the young child's fantasy play is based on emotional familiarity. The goodness of mealtimes is repeated in fantasy again and again! The five- through seven-year-olds demonstrate the developing cortex, the region of conceptual thought. Whereas before the fifth year, an idea for a game is sparked by an object in the environment, after this time, the ideas begin to emerge from within. All this critical development is fostered best in the traditional way, through robust, creative child's play.

The human spirit needs these years to be grounded in a healthy balanced environment, created by healthy balanced adults who love the child. This offers the child the best potential to develop a whole brain/whole body, çnely integrated system, to stand as a foundation for the lifework of the spirit. In this way, "The soul-spirit individuality can ... begin to manifest itself fully in an external way through this body, without being hindered by it."

Sharifa Oppenheimer

Tasks and Goals for Parents and Educators

I F WE WISH TO UNDERSTAND A CHILD in the first seven years of life, we must look very closely at the individual steps of development. Before we do this however, let us keep in mind the whole situation of the small child at the beginning of life.

To begin with, three things must coincide if a birth is to happen. First the two streams of inheritance of the parents unite to give the body. A soul-spirit being, a human individuality then joins with the body.

For instance, in spite of its outer completeness, this physical body still remains unfinished in many ways. The individual inner organs have not yet attained their final, differentiated form. In the limb system, we see a lack of differentiation—chaotic, involuntary movements. In the nerve-sense system, the child is still totally open.

Children's task in the first six to seven years—years that are theirs by right for this purpose—is to take hold of their inner body and to develop its differentiation until they are ready for school. Then—when the process of forming the organs is largely finished and only growth is still taking place—

the body stands prepared as a useful "instrument." The soul-spirit individuality that had joined the physical body at birth can, after further steps of development, begin to manifest itself fully in an external way through this body without being hindered by it.

How can we observe the joining of the individuality to the body? We see how the child's involuntary movements of kicking about gradually become more ordered and directed through the tireless will to be active. We see how the child acquires the upright position and develops a relationship to the world's equilibrium in learning to walk. We observe how from the world-wide language of babbling a small child finds the way ever more surely and with greater control to the exact sound of the regional language. We see how a much more strongly differentiated and more meaningful activity develops from the early toddling about after adults and the beginning imitation of their behavior.

We can see through all these processes how the individuality is endeavoring to work itself into the body and to make it its own. All the impressions from the environment that meet the child also work very closely in this process of shaping the inner human being.

The impressions work in from the outside through the senses. In the small child these are digested inwardly by the core being, the individuality, in two ways: through imitated behavior and in the development of the yet unfinished organs.

The small child is born unprotected into its new environment. The whole body acts as a single sense organ serving in an indiscriminate way to join the outer world with the inner one. We can compare it to the eye. The eye itself does not see, it only transmits. We see through the eyes. Thus the child's body is a sense organ for the individuality, for the spirit-soul being of the human.

The outer impressions come into the child through the senses, while the inner activity of shaping the organs, moves outwards. This working together of the outer impressions and the inner shaping manifests itself in that wonderful power of imitation with which each healthy child is born. Every observation is first taken in deeply, grasped by the will and then, like an echo, comes forth again in a child's behavior.

There result from this fact two significant tasks for parents and educators. The first is a gesture of protection. Wherever we are able to do so, we ought to choose carefully out of the environment the impressions that meet the child. The child is best surrounded calmly by happy family sounds of normal speaking and singing rather than those of uproar and quarreling. We also ought to protect the very young child as much as possible from technical apparatus such as radio, television, cassettes, videos, etc. In the child's room, cradles and walls of one, soft color, because of their soothing effect, are preferable to the well-meant but overstimulating "children's" fabrics and wallpaper which are covered with bright flowers and animals. When riding in the car, the child can be seated to have a view of mother.

The second great task consists in guiding children step by step into life, allowing them to learn about life for their whole life. This happens chiefly by meaningfully and methodically paying attention to the capability that children bring with them—that of imitation—rather than by means of clever teaching.

This presupposes that when we as grown-ups make the effort to be good "examples" of human beings, we will have the effect of awakening impulses in the child through our activities. For we cannot teach a child to imitate. This is a matter of the will and must be grasped by the child's own will. We can be aware of our own behavior: how we go about our work in the home and garden, how we speak with other people, how we care for others, how we arrange and care for our environment. Children take everything deeply into their own bodily formative processes. Without being able to discriminate between meaningful or foolish behavior, they bring to their own activity what they see in their representatives of life, which is the role we take on in the process of education.

The imitative behavior of the child goes through three different stages in the first six to seven years. It is subject to the forces forming the organs, which—beginning in the head area—work through the whole body right down to the tips of the toes. Although they work through the whole body, they concentrate in the first stage of life, from birth to about two-and-a-half years of age, on the forming of the nerve-sense system. During this time the child acquires three of the most important human capabilities—gaining uprightness in the face of gravity, walking, and then speech, which is a prerequisite for thinking. All these capabilities the child learns exclusively through imitation. Tragic examples in history have shown that children do not acquire these human capabilities when they grow up surrounded only by animals. This shows clearly that humanity can only be learned from human beings.

From the Age of Crawling to the Awakening of the "I" in the Age of Independence

In what way are children active in this first stage of life?

As soon as they can barely crawl or propel themselves forward, they begin to explore their home environment, and it becomes unsafe. They follow mother and want to do everything that she is doing. With the greatest enjoyment they clatter together the cooking pots, covers and spoons, put their hands into the wash water, pull out the wash and stick it in again, spreading puddles about. They bustle around with the broom, dispersing the dirt rather than gathering it into the middle in a small pile; they eagerly carry things that have just been placed in a certain spot to some other spot. And all this is done with the motto, "Johnny, too" or "Me, too!" They take great joy in moving and busying themselves as much as possible with real household items, yet without insight into the purpose and goal of the adult's work—which, of course, progresses very slowly. Without such "willing helpers" the adult work would be done much sooner. However, this is true only from one point of view, for the parent has taken care not only of the house, garden or handwork, but at the same time she has also accomplished educational work. This should become recognized again much more in today's educational awareness.

Along with their impulsive engagement with the environment, there are also moments when children linger devotedly near mother—for example, when she is peeling apples or working with needle and thread. There are times when they busy themselves in the play area—filling up baskets and emptying them, building towers and knocking them down, singing and pushing a doll carriage. Here it is important to pay close attention to the quality of the play materials. The best objects are those found in nature or which have been only slightly shaped by hand (*Toymaking with Children*, Freya Jaffke). In their close connection with these objects, the impressions made upon the children will be natural, organic shapes, and this works to stimulate their inner organ-forming processes. "Toys with dead mathematical forms alone have a desolating and killing effect upon a child's formative forces" (*The Education of the Child*, Rudolf Steiner).

Children pass through their first real crisis point when for the first time the feeling of "I" is awakened during the Age of Defiance. They experience their own will more and more, but must now learn to bring it into harmony with their environment. Whereas earlier the child always called out "Me, too," now the child says, "I don't want to."

From the Third to the Fifth Year: Fantasy and Spontaneous Play

Let us now take a look at the second stage, the time between about the third to fifth year. The life or formative forces, which until now have chiefly been at work in the head region, concentrate in this second stage in the middle part of the body, where most importantly the rhythmical organs (heart and lungs) are located. At this time, two quite new capabilities appear in children, which clearly give them a new relationship to their environment. These capabilities are: a childlike fantasy and memory.

Here are some examples of play in children who have developed in a healthy way:

A four-year-old has small round pieces of real tree branches in front of him on the table and he asks me, "Do you want soda, beer or apple juice?"

A four-year-old girl takes a piece of bark, lays two stones upon it and says, "I have a ship with a man at the wheel." Then she comes to my table and asks, "I have brought you some pieces of chocolate, do you want them?" and she lays the stones in front of me. And now the bark becomes a roof for a small dwarf's house.

A small bench is first a doll's stove; lying on its side it becomes an animal's feeding trough, and upside down it is a doll's bed, and then part of a train.

These examples show that children of this age are capable of changing things in their environment, using them for different purposes in certain cases and, with the help of fantasy, making them into new things. Children see objects, perhaps remembering them only vaguely, and their imagination fills in all the other necessary details. The prerequisite is that children have already experienced such things before. If a child has never seen a ship, or only seen one in a picture book, she cannot bring it into her play.

A characteristic of play at this age is that it is stimulated by external causes. For this reason, it is best if the available play materials are capable of transformation by being incomplete and simple enough so that a child's imagination, remembering the details, can transcend the available objects and fill them in. The imagination needs this type of activity in order not to become stagnant. Everything depends on the inner work.

As the muscles of the hand grow firm and strong in performing the work for which they are fitted, so the brain and other organs of the human physical body are guided into the right lines of development if they receive the right impression from the environment (*The Education of the Child*, Rudolf Steiner).

It is immediately striking that the play is full of change. There are always daily events that are imitated and there are many spontaneous changes—often without any connection. Children continuously think of something new. Many adults who see this may despair and believe children are unable to concentrate in their play. Concentration at this age level, however, lies in the continuity of play which between three and five years old is characterized in this way. To be sure, quite a bit of disorder and even chaos arises now and then from this play. But it can be called meaningful chaos for it continuously affects children in such a way that they remain stimulated and interested. By the fifth year, this already changes on its own. Of course, after the playtime, the adult should plan sufficient time to clean up, participating to set an example so that it becomes an indisputable and joyful habit rather than a sporadically ordered, almost overwhelming burden which one faces alone.

From the Fifth to the Seventh Year: Pictures from the Imagination and Planned Play

The third big developmental step of the first seven years begins around the fifth year. The forces that have been used to form the organs are being freed more and more from the rhythmical system and are now working in the metabolic-limb system. The children are increasingly capable and dexterous right down to their fingertips.

Many children—especially those who were able to play in a rich and creative manner—go through a second crisis in the fifth year. For the first time they experience real boredom. They can stand before you and say, "I don't know what to do." It is as if their fantasy has left them and suddenly they have no more ideas. Fantasy needs a rest now and ought not to be called upon by reminding the child of yesterday's fine play. We can help to strengthen it much more by having the child participate in our own work—for example, peeling apples, drying dishes, sweeping, baking, sewing. After a while, sometimes after only a few days, new impulses for their play arise in the child. A change has taken place. The stimulus for play no longer comes so much from external objects, but it comes now more and more from inside. This means that now the children have an inner picture, a picture from their imagination of past events and they can bring these up in their play independent of place, time or people.

Five- and six-year-old children love to crouch together talking and making plans for their play. For example, they are building an inn and folded cloths become napkins, menus and purses. A cold buffet is set up and little woolen sheep are offered as fish. One child who is selling drinks has a large log with small branches on it standing before him (it is his "real beer keg"), and he is able to fill an order for any kind of drink with it. Another time they set up a doctor's office with needles, stethoscopes, bandages and a waiting room where the folded cloths serve as magazines.

Other typical themes of play are: trash truck, ambulance with a red light, school, carpentry shop, fire engine, cable-railway, telephone installation, deepsea diver, and much more. Their play becomes more and more planned. This does not mean, however, that it can't be suddenly changed in the middle if one of the children comes up with a rousing idea.

Children of this age do not need fancier, more detailed play things. Play materials that can grow with them are better. Their relationship to the materials is changing. Before the fifth year an idea is stimulated by the materials. After the fifth year an imaginative idea comes first, then comes an effort to find and make something acceptable from the play materials that corresponds to the imagination. Now the fantasy, which had been so richly developed before, begins to function again.

Nowadays it is no longer a matter of course that children can play so spontaneously and enthusiastically at their corresponding level of development. This is due less to the children than to the immense influence from all sides upon them from earliest childhood on. For example, fully detailed, technically exact toys make it difficult for children to be satisfied with such outwardly simple things as objects from nature, cloths, wooden branches, etc. A healthy child would rather be right in the middle of play than outside as an observer of perfect, technical instruments. The fascination for such toys is soon past and leaves behind both an emptiness and a longing for more.

The unspoken reward and thanks for such efforts come to the adult through children who are able to play in a fulfilling way and who are building the basis for later life in these early stages. One of our most important tasks is to arrange the space—at home and in the kindergarten—to guarantee the needs of creative play. Above all this means creating a world suitable for imitation with adults who are active in a purposeful way, who like to do their work, and who, at the same time, accompany the children in their play in a quiet way. Creative play depends more on a calm, joyful atmosphere of work than on many clever words, suggestions for play or instructions of any kind. The children must be "lifted up" by the adults' work, they must have a place in it in the broadest sense—even if they are not directly involved in the work. This seems like a contradiction, but it can be experienced by every mother and every father who radiates calm and interest while working in the home. The most important thing is the people who surround the child—that they make life rhythmical and ordered, that they like to work and are ready to take on a large part of the work themselves. The small child is an imitator!

In retrospect, the tasks of the educator can easily be discovered from all the above descriptions. If we look at the goals, we can summarize by saying that nothing more wonderful can happen in childhood than that a child is able to grasp completely each developmental step, pass though it in a healthy way, and to practice and gain strength during each particular challenge. When the body is completely formed and accomplishes its first change around age seven, children may turn to schoolwork with the same joy, strength and enthusiasm for learning that they showed earlier for play and be equal to its demands.

Freya Jaffke

2. Kindergarten Education with Mixed-Age Groups

The mixed-age kindergarten offers remarkable benefits to all the children of the varying ages. Certainly for the younger children there is a wealth of skills modeled by their older classmates, whether social, motor, imaginative, verbal or emotional. They also have the advantage of a curriculum of stories, poems, games and rhymes that challenge them to stretch their capacities. The added incentive of wanting to join their elders in the fun can, through the wonder of imitation, make this learning easier. It is a tremendous experience to offer Circle Time to a mixed-age group, in which some of the material is designed for the more developed skills of the older children. It is as though the younger ones are carried along in the current of the older children's enthusiasm, and through imitation they can join whole-heartedly.

For older children in a mixed-age group, the benefits are, perhaps, more interior. They have the opportunity to look backward a bit and see the path they have recently trod. They also have the occasion to ground their learning in action. It is very satisfying for the child who can button her own coat, to turn and help the smaller one beside her. As adults we know it is a great advantage to teach others what we have just learned. It takes the learning out of the realm of passive knowledge and makes it active and accessible. Also, in teaching others, one is required to break down the action into simple steps. This, the older ones learn to do intuitively, following the old saying "little steps for little feet." It is also very helpful for the older children to have the opportunity to learn compassion, patience and tolerance for the little one's still-developing behaviors. They learn to demonstrate love in action through these qualities.

In a mixed-age group, it is an excellent life lesson to find that people with differing developmental abilities have different standards set for them. Behaviors that are overlooked in the younger children would never be accepted in the more mature children. And the older children can be given privileges that the younger ones need to grow into. In this way the older children can measure their own growth, and the younger ones can stretch toward a goal. As we will see in the richly detailed descriptions of this article, the children of differing ages make relationship to the classroom work, and all kindergarten activities, in their own developmentally specific ways.

Waldorf Education is a social education. In a mixed-age group, the child has the benefit of living into the variety of human capacity and experience. This deepens, rounds out, and fosters the child's own growing capabilities.

The foundation of this rests on the teacher's own imagination and inner versatility. A mixed-age group requires that the teacher continue to strive, to know appropriate materials for all the ages in her group, to have a sense of the developmental course of each child, and to be able to address each of these when needed throughout the day. This is not only a great challenge for the teacher, but it is a great blessing as well. When the teacher strives, in this way, the children are given the gift of absorbing, heart to heart, this essential human quality. Much of the "teaching" takes place between the children themselves also, as an older child shows the younger one how to fold the napkin or coaches her in socially acceptable ways to have her needs met, "Let's take turns!"

The teacher's inner attitude, her attention to her work, the order she establishes in the room, the rhythm of the day, her awareness of the whole group as well as each individual child, all of these are qualities the child imbibes through imitation. These characteristics will live deeply into the child's being, and in the future this gift will be returned to the world as the young adult steps into life.

Sharifa Oppenheimer

I N THIS ARTICLE AN EXAMPLE WILL be given of how the type of preschool education for which we aim is feasible, particularly when the children's group is composed not only of one age group (five- and six–year-old children), but rather of three to four age groups (three-, four-, five-, and six-year-old children). To what extent the adult masters the necessary differentiations of the various age levels and satisfies the different needs of the children depends largely, to be sure, upon his or her imagination and inner versatility.

In such a mixed-age group, the children live together as in a large family. They learn from one another and help one another in a way that is rarely necessary or done among those of the same age. It is even quite realistic for the three-year-olds to experience that the six-year-olds may be allowed to do things that they are not yet allowed to do; and, conversely, the three-year-olds are excused from things that would not be tolerated with the six-year-olds.

If one wishes to lay a foundation for later ability in life during the preschool years, one cannot do better than to have children learn about the diversity of life. However, it is the adult's task to choose from the fullness of life what is particularly beneficial for the different developmental levels of the children. On the other hand, she will not attempt to introduce too early certain activities (especially in the intellectual domain) so that the development does not proceed in a one-sided manner.

The way children learn from life reveals itself in their urge to participate in all activities or events in their environment, joining in immediately or carrying them out by imitating them in play. This is, however, only possible

when these activities can be looked at and experienced in connection with real life. Therefore, it is the educator's duty to include whenever possible the necessary work of daily life in the kindergarten plan. Some examples: housework—cooking, baking, washing, ironing, sweeping, dusting, and flower care; toymaking and toy care—to this belong, among other things, sawing, rasping, cutting,

gluing, repairs of all kinds, sewing, and mending; garden work—digging, sowing, planting, watering, weeding, mowing, and harvesting. In addition, there are experiences on walks, for example, encountering rubbish trucks, street workers, gardeners, the workers in the adjacent childcare center.

Nevertheless, the quantity of experiences is not of primary concern, but rather that the children can experience the work as well as the attitude of the people doing the work—how they perform the various jobs one after the other, and how they work hand in hand helping one another. All this will be taken by the child—not with the intellect in an evaluating, critical or reflective way, but with her entire being which is so capable of surrendering itself to experiences. In this way impulses for her own activity and practice are awakened, and, simultaneously, the forces that build up and form the body are stimulated in various ways.

From these developments arise the guiding principles for the educator's methodology in the preschool years. The teacher will work together with the children in significant, necessary ways so that the children can take up the work directly and be imitative in their activity. She will not, however, teach this information about life in a scholarly fashion. The aimed-for method is comprised of a well thought out and richly endowed education of opportunities that, however, leaves quite open:

1) what the respective child grasps by imitating;

2) how the child imitates the activity, according to age (from three- to six-years-old);

3) which results will arise from the imitation in the developmental progress of the individual child.

It is not necessary to have extensively prepared activity times in which the children are restrained and told, now and not later, this and not that, this long and not longer or shorter, together with these children and not alone in that corner.

The imitative ability and differentiation in this respect depend upon quite definite suppositions:

1) about the way the adults shape the world to be imitated;

2) about the age of the child within the first seven years; and

3) about the individuality of each child.

In the following example of different work situations (in a group of twenty-three children from three- to six-years-old), the explanations should become clear. Such work happens during the children's free play time and consequently becomes an organic part of the daily and weekly rhythm of the kindergarten.

The gardener gives us a freshly cut birch tree and from it we want to saw new pieces of wood for building. The five- and six-year-old boys immediately take the meter-long pieces of trunk, lay cloths underneath and push the wood like a train over the floor and under tables draped with cloths (tunnels). Other six-year-olds are again nearby, helping and competing with one another as to who can work up the most sweat. After a while, Jan and Markus, both six years old, begin to build a railroad through the whole room with tables placed one behind the other. The three- and four-year-olds, as patient passengers, get on and off the train at the conductor's order. Suddenly, the big children notice that the saw's noise fits well with their railroad, and so we agree to be attentive to one another. First we go slowly, then faster, then slowly again, then a pause. With great enthusiasm the engineers look out of their window to the carpenter's bench and follow with close attention how quickly the saw goes through the wood. Shortly before the block of wood falls off, it seems that they hold their breath and in the next moment breathe out again forcefully shouting out the station's name with joy. The conductor urges the passengers to hurry, for he notices that the pauses made by the saw do not last very long.

Under the carpenter's bench eager hands are gathering the sawdust and pieces of bark. Markus, four years old, takes it as feed for his horse; Gernot, four, lets it snow in the room; Tanja, five, bakes a birthday cake out of it and decorates it with fruit pits from the store. Next to the pieces of wood which are yet to be sawed, Mathias, Aureha and Susanne, all four years old, are standing and saying, "Here you can make a bridge out of it, and that would be a good coffee can, and look, if you saw off some here, it will be a little house with a chimney; and, look, that looks like a dog." They use some  longer branches as a flute, violin and cello and move through the room playing music with them. Shortly afterwards, they carry the branches on their shoulders by twos and offer "apple juice" for sale from the buckets hanging in the middle. But the variety of possible uses for their branches is still not exhausted. They also serve as walking sticks, ski poles, and finally—furnished with a crocheted band—as bow and arrows.

Next to the carpenter's bench, Georgia, three years old, is standing with a doll under her arm. Delighted, she waits anew each piece of wood that is sawed off, falls down or is ably snapped up by a bigger child. In between she brings single blocks to Helge, six, and Michael, six, who are building in the corner with bark and big pieces of wood.

After the sawing work is done, the remaining branches will be dragged outside, the carpenter's bench pushed against the wall, the work things cleaned up and the sawdust swept together.

It is now time for the breakfast preparation. There is muesli, and the apples for it must be peeled. Stephen, three, stands next to me and enjoys the long peels which may be eaten. He then goes into the playhouse and tells the other children, "We have already peeled the apples." Cornelia and Aurelia, both four years old, would also like to peel such a long peel but barely succeed in going once around the apple. Eventually, they have finished peeling an apple all the way. Their great satisfaction lasts for several weeks. They like to imitate this activity in imaginative play, for example, by wrapping a crocheted band around a block of wood for the apple peel and letting a piece of bark be the knife. The "work" is quickly finished in this way, and the imagination has the possibility of using the same items in another way by letting the band be the shores of a lake and the bark a little ship; or the band is wrapped around a big piece of bark to become a stringed instrument—a kantalina. Jan, Michael and Antje, all six years old, notice that I peel the apple in a spiral and that in this way the peel becomes very long. They are unable to do it the same way and do not stop until all the apples are peeled. During this whole time, Ulrike, six, was busy sewing. She has put a pin cushion, scissors, thimble and material scraps into the little basket and taken it into her "house." She has knotted herself a little doll and, in addition, has sewn two pillows. She has allowed nothing to disturb her, not even Dietmar, five, who has requested several times that she try on a pair of fur shoes in this shoemaker's workshop.

This small glimpse into a play and work situation of a mixed-age children's group already shows how differently the individual children participate in adult work, how they act according to their age, and how many possibilities for differentiation can arise. Thereby, three very different developmental stages can be recognized, the knowledge of which is a necessary presupposition for the stimulation of the children. For playing and being purposefully active need to be relearned today by many children, especially when they come into the kindergarten for the first time at age five and have not had opportunities beforehand to play imaginatively.

In the first developmental stage, which is just ending for many children as they begin their kindergarten time, a large change in activity can be observed. They watch, help out, in some cases let themselves be included in a game by the older children, and for moments become absorbed in play to the extent that they forget everything about them. The activity of the four-year-olds is also defined by a large change, but now it is through their developing and often exuberant imagination. However, a prerequisite for this is a toy selection that is kept so simple that it stimulates the imagination as well as allows for transformation of the toys themselves. After the fifth year, when children have more imagination and memory capability at their disposal, the spontaneous activity is organized gradually into purposeful activity. When several children of this older group are together, the play is mostly a question of a project that will be logically accomplished. This does not preclude that spontaneous ideas can arise and totally change the play situation again and again. However, the play of these older kindergarten children is usually goal-oriented and resolute.

Difficult situations can also be overcome if, as an educator, one bears in mind how the children's behavior is based on age.

For instance, during clean-up time after free play time, the three- and four-year-olds are either busy beside the adults or "thoughtlessly" busy, for they do not yet quite understand the correlation and purpose of this activity. In certain cases, with the best of intentions, they move things that have just been put away in the correct place to another place.

The four- and five-year-olds eagerly help out, but often make a game out of cleaning up and need much encouragement. When we can manage it, it suits the child well if we build a picture, for example: "You can now be the farmer who is bringing all the animals back to their stalls from the pasture," instead of the abstract order, "Now put the animals back on the shelf." When four- and five-year-olds, for example, pick up building blocks, fold cloths or bring chairs to their places, it often happens that they do it in very creative ways stimulated by their rich imaginations. As mother does at home when ironing, the cloths are slowly pulled over the edges of the tables or "ironed" with a small, turned-over stool. The chairs will perhaps be carried on their shoulders, because they are just being brought in from the "carpenter's," or they are pushed in a row in front of them as a train. The building blocks will be laid, for example, on a slope to a basket after being hoisted up, because they have just become dump trucks or ship loaders.

The five- and six-year-old children can already distance themselves from the play and independently accomplish a task requested of them. They either choose for themselves an area that they want to clean up alone, or they ask the adults for a job. In general, they pay very close attention to how the adult does the work and try to do it as carefully and as well. For example, they fold cloths very neatly or arrange the baskets in the building or shopping corner. They have an overview of the work sequence and its logic that they acquire through the repetition of doing it again and again during the year, and they can give a hand independent of the adults. Thus, they already fetch the broom and dustpan for sweeping when the building corner is barely finished being picked up.

Such differentiations in the various age levels are represented in all activities that take place in the daily life of the children's group. Each child can normally fulfill the developmental stages appropriate for him or her in such a group situation. The modeling effect of the children on each other in the mixed-age group is also invaluable. The concern that perhaps the five- and six-year-old children would not come into their own in a mixed-age group—that they would be hindered in their continued development—is only justified when the actual group includes more than twenty to twenty-three children, and when, because of space limitations, play that requires a lot of room is not possible. After these outer considerations, however, all else depends on the inner activity with which the adult carries out her work. For this is also perceptible to the children and, therefore, is imitable and helps the children learn to evolve their own initiatives.

Later in life, much will depend upon what type of experiences children encountered in the first six or seven years. For what is germinated in these early developmental stages must appear one way or another in a later stage. Thus, abilities and deficiencies can occur in many areas. For example, children who have been allowed to absorb, by imitating, purposeful and understandable work from their environment will, as adults, have a command over such abilities on an intellectual level; they will have at their disposal as adults logic in their thinking. All that a child perceives in the working adult and can practice by imitating—like consciousness, attention, order, purposeful results of work—is accompanied by intensive experience. With this, the experiences go into deeper levels, which later can be stirred from the consciousness and can assist in an independent, goal-directed shaping of one's life. Children will be able to follow the teacher's words with greater alertness and concentration if they have had the opportunity in every respect, especially in their limbs, to attain numerous skills. In this way, children will be able to control their movements. They can then achieve an outer calm and increase more and more of their inner activity. Of course, in addition to the capabilities, which, as indicated, are transformed, there are also some which intensify in a linear manner.

The work of the adult and the transformation of the work throughout the children's play have been depicted here. Artistic activities (eurythmy, painting, modeling, music-making), storytelling and outdoor play are, of course, equally important components in the total educational work. In each of these activities there could also be shown both the specific formative value of the activity and the differentiations according to age levels.

Freya Jaffke,
Germany, Waldorf
Kindergarten Association

3. The Significance of Imitation in the Development of the Will

The power of imitation is a dual process, one that incorporates the opposites: the receptive process of taking in through the senses, and the active process of taking hold of this sense information by the will. When a child is born, much of the organism is as yet unformed, not yet rhythmical. It is through this taking in by the senses and taking hold by the will that the spirit of the child is able to complete a physical form, a body that will serve it well for its purpose on earth.

As we saw in an earlier article, the physical environment must be arranged in order that the child's senses are fostered by an "opening into" the world. The child will take in whatever exists in the environment, but if what is offered is harsh, over-stimulating, mechanical, electronic, violent, and so forth, then the natural organic response is for the senses to close down.

Let's remember the three essentials for learning: sense experience, emotionally responsive movement, and the ability to imitate what is modeled in the environment. If the sense experience is such that the organ closes down, learning is significantly hampered.

For instance, noise pollution may be to such a degree that the fine hair-like receptors in the inner ear are damaged, and the child thereby loses the ability to hear tones in the upper register. When these high tones are heard properly, the

areas of the brain that foster concentration and focus are stimulated. A child exposed to loud music or machines may lose the organic underpinning of these essential qualities. Some new therapies are beginning to work with sound and tone, to help the brain integrate.

If movement is restricted, by the use of electronic media or television or even by early emphasis on academic learning, again, an essential requirement for learning, for making the world meaningful, is hindered. Even in babyhood, modern children can become movement-deprived. Rather than being laid on a blanket on the floor and allowed to wriggle, stretch, and roll, babies are strapped into ultra-cushioned reclining seats where they spend hours. All the balance, core muscle development, and movement exploration essential in learning to walk can be damaged by baby-walkers. Our modern preoccupation with "safety" can so heavily restrict free exploratory movement, that it becomes "unsafe" for the child's overall development.

If a young child's capacity to imitate is overwhelmed by overly instructed and structured activities, this essential component is weakened. Kindergarten teachers notice in their students, a reduced innate capacity for imitation, due to media influence, as well. The finest possible environment to foster the child's ability to imitate is the realm of creative play. In this article, we see beautiful examples of the way the adult's work offers stimulation not only for imitation, but for sparkling flights of imagination.

A critical element in this formula is the human adult, one worthy of imitation. It is essential that we create outer environments that allow for and encourage the children's wide palette of sense experience, as well as their ability to respond with purposeful movement, and also foster their natural need to imitate. But we must also attend to the inner environment, our own sense of order, rhythm, purpose, and will, as well as our own emotional tenor throughout the day.

Sharifa Oppenheimer

TODAY WE WILL TALK ABOUT THE DEVELOPMENT of the will, and we will see how important it is that the child has an example to imitate. We all know that children have a great openness and are entirely sense organ. All of their sense impressions go deeply into the body. They can't defend themselves from sense impressions, which flood into them.

But a sense organ is only an instrument, which can be used by someone. The eye itself, for example, does not see. Someone must look through the eye to see. The eye is only an instrument for seeing. In order to see, the will within the human being must be at work. The whole physical body is one great sense organ for the spiritual and soul being of the child, which came from a pre-earthly existence.

Now we can see two phenomena: First the child is totally a sense being, and second, the child is totally a will being. With the will and through the senses all the impressions from the environment are grasped and taken deeply into the body where they leave their marks upon the organs. The synthesis of these two phenomena is seen in the wonderful forces of imitation, which every child brings as a gift from pre-birth existence. In the pre-earthly life the human soul is living among cosmic beings, is penetrated by them and follows them. This "habit" is taken through the gate of birth into early childhood and is seen in the forces of imitation. The child's imitation is a double process: receiving through the senses, and grasping and imitating with the will. Rudolf Steiner describes the development of the will in *The Education of the Child* (pp. 33-34):

"By a proper application of fundamental educational principles during the first seven years of childhood the foundation is laid for the development of a strong and healthy will; for a strong and healthy will must have its support in well-developed forms of the physical body."

We know that all the organs of the young child are relatively unshaped. They do not yet have the physical form that one sees in the organs of the adult, and the rhythm of each organ is not yet developed. We must ask ourselves, "How does the forming of the organs take place and how will they develop their rhythm and their rhythmical working together?" A seemingly different, but related question is, "How will it happen that the will of the child becomes purposeful and orderly?" Both happen primarily through the influences from the world outside the child, especially through all the rhythmical events during the day or week that appear repeatedly at the same time.

This is a summary of the lecture that Freya Jaffke presented at a North American Kindergarten conference at High Mowing School in New Hampshire. The summary was written from her lecture notes and may differ somewhat from the lecture as it was given.

Now let us look at the period of the first three years of life. There we can see that children have many possibilities to use and exercise their will forces, though of course this happens unconsciously. What a great activity of will is involved when a small child slowly comes into the upright and acquires the ability to walk! Then the child follows mother through the house "working" with her, doing some laundry, cleaning the floor, packing and unpacking the grocery basket. The more the mother does her work in good order and without being hectic, the more the child's will is guided in a strong direction. In this way, children learn to move their limbs with more and more coordination.

Everything children do is done without reflection or consideration. They do it out of imitation and habit. The quality of example will determine how habits develop, and in the same way children will experience their limits. If the adult only laughs when a child, for example, dumps spinach from the plate onto the table, or pulls on the tablecloth or the cord of the iron, then the child learns bad habits and develops an unhealthy will orientation. The adult should think ahead! The adult should use imagination or fantasy to divert the child from activities that are inappropriate. The adult should be consequent and follow through to establish limits. This means that the  adult has to be a representative of everything for the child, so that the child has a clear orientation and a sense of reality. It is important that the children are always surrounded by meaningful will activities as long as they are unable to guide themselves.

The first real crisis occurs when children experience their own will for the first time. Then they begin to use the word "I" for themselves and the word "no" to others. At the same time they experience a conflict between their growing will and the will of those around them. Their own will can only show itself in relation to the will of the others in their environment. Children have to slowly learn to bring their will into a harmonious relationship with the will of those around them. Here again we can see how wonderful and healthy are good habits and rhythms in the child's environment. It is especially during these years that they can help to overcome many difficult situations.

During this first period of early childhood the will of the child was engaged through a strong connection to the mother's activities. Now in the second period between the third and fifth years of age, the will becomes more and more connected to the awakening imagination and begins to work within the children's fantasy. During this period, their fantasy needs the inspiration of the objects in their environment. For example, the child sees a piece of bark and a few stones and takes them to be a boat with people; or a doll and starts to feed it; or a little bench and uses it as a mailbox. The will within the child's fantasy is able to transform things, and the child no longer needs only actual

(realistic) objects. But the object has to be simple enough to allow space for this creative activity. The objects in the child's environment spark the fantasy. Children feel great joy and freedom through creating new things that for them are real. An example of how children transform items from their environment into play materials is the following: The mother has prepared a large package, and she puts the leftover piece of string over the back of a chair. The child ties a wooden spoon to one end and pulls at the other end to make a crane.

Between three and five we can see that the child's fantasy and the child's faculty of memory appear at the same time. Only things or events can be remembered that have been seen before. How does a child remember? How does fantasy, which is the bringing together of a memory picture and an object, actually occur? And then, how does the child carry this fantasy into creative play? The answer is through the will forces. Without the will forces nothing will happen. If the will forces are chaotic, nothing meaningful happens in the child's play. Thus we see how important it is to care for the right development of the will.

Healthy and harmonious children always have new ideas to bring to the same materials or the same play. They are always active, always busy with their will. For example, the little bench that was the mailbox now becomes the manger for the animals, a bed for the doll, a stove, or many other things. We are all familiar with the difficult and inharmonious children who are not able to play but like to disturb the others. We also have those children who don't do anything, but just stand around looking at the others. They seem to be apathetic. These children especially need to experience, for a shorter or longer time, the meaningful work of an adult as well as the strong rhythm and the warm atmosphere of the kindergarten.

Around the fifth year, a second crisis is to be seen, mostly in the children who until now were always busy and knew just what to do. What is happening now? The fantasy apparently disappears; the will seems to be paralyzed. A child may say, "I don't know what to do today," or "I'm bored." A big inner change is taking place. At this time it is important that we not appeal to the fantasy forces, for they now need a quiet time. We shouldn't say, "Yesterday you built up such a beautiful landscape, do it again." Instead, let them do real things, such as making a little book with drawings for their dolls, sewing a felt holder for needles, or sanding a letter opener that you have just carved.

It is important that all these activities have a strong connection to the adult's work. It is still the period of imitation, but we can more and more use words in guiding the child to an activity. We can ask them to come and help us in our work, but not with questions! If we want them to help in the kitchen with cooking and baking we should say, "Come, give me a hand," rather than "Will you give me a hand?" After a short time of such working, new impulses will arise, impulses for the child's own play.

At this new stage of development, around the fifth year, there arise within children a picture or mental image of what they want to do. Now the will forces have to join or enter into the mental image. That requires much effort. The child is still in the kindergarten, and the play materials have not changed. When plans arise in the mental image, such as a hairdresser's shop, an ambulance, a fishing boat, or a restaurant, then the child needs to be able to call upon the well-trained fantasy of the years before. And the child needs patience, enthusiasm and staying power. These are all faculties in which the will works strongly.

Before five the stimulus for play comes from the outside. A child sees a curved stick and says, "Now I am a chimney sweeper." After five the child says, "I would like to be a chimney sweeper, and I need a broom with a long handle." The child looks for something similar, sees feathers, puts them together, attaches a long curved ribbon and is happy. Before five, the will activity works with what stimulates the fantasy from the outside. After five, the will forces have to make an inner effort. The will now joins together with the mental image and joins also with the well-trained fantasy. Thus the children create new objects that appear in their mental image without the need for an outer stimulus.

At this point in children's development we may think that they must do strong physical work such as sawing, nailing and hammering. They may do such work, but we shouldn't forget that the will forces have to be exercised not only within the muscles, but at this particular period of life, they have to also grow strong within the inner being of the child. They are needed within the mental image.

Here are two examples of play situations that show you how we can help children during their play, as of course, children do need help sometimes. Florian, age six years, four months, plays that he is a circus director. He dresses many children as different animals with various cloths. He tells them what to do and where to stay. All of them are happy and follow his lead for a period of time. When he has no more ideas and some "animals" have already left, I tell him, "The circus is now finished and all the circus people must have a snack." Florian replies, "Yes, and then they will pack everything and go to another town. Oh yes, this could be my circus-wagon. A circus wagon always has a round roof, doesn't it?"

The object he points to has previously been a "cage" and stood beneath the table where I was working. He builds up his "wagon," then looks out of his little window at me and says, "Oh, I am already close to the border! Now I am going to drive into another country and there will be a large amount of snow, and there one needs a snowplow." Then he fixes a little wooden dust pan to the front of his wagon as a snowplow. In the back he builds up something for spreading salt. He uses little benches with small holes on the top for carrying. He stacks them one on top of the other and through the holes he throws chestnuts with great joy.

On the next day, Florian again builds up a wagon, but this time without snowplow or salt machine. When he is finished he says, "Now it is a locomotive." Then he builds up two more wagons behind. Other children want to play with him but do not really know what to do. I say, "One wagon could be for my luggage, and some porters could come to get my suitcases, for I have to travel. The other wagon can be the dining room, for I would like to eat something during my journey." A great "busyness" arises among the children. Some of them carry all my cases (big logs) to the train. Others set up the tables in the dining car. I am given a menu out of folded cloths and have to choose and to order. Then they bring wonderful dishes and set my table. I am totally integrated into the play of the children, although I am still sitting at my work table. They do not mind at all that I am not sitting with them in the dining car, as I do sometimes.

I think we are lucky to have some children every year who are able to play in such a fulfilled way. They stimulate the others. Another example is Simon, age six, who has built a camping place underneath a table. After he is finished, nothing more happens. Then I say, "In a camping place, there is always a fireplace where people cook their meals." "Oh yes, may we get some sticks?" I reply, "Yes, take three." They attach the sticks together to make three legs. With red and yellow cloths, they make a fire underneath. A little basket is fixed in the middle of the sticks. It is the cooking pot. They ask for two more sticks, put them between two chairs, put big cloths over them and make tents. Within the tents they have woolen carpets and cushions. These activities last until clean-up time. Then the boys are a little disappointed because "they haven't played yet."

The question is: What can the adult do to help strengthen the will forces as they appear in these play situations? If indeed, as Rudolf Steiner says, it is from the outside that the impressions on the organs come about, and also the well-developed forms of the organs are the best support for the will, then in the environment there must be order in manifold ways—rhythm, good habits and love. To come to an appropriate order around the children, the adult has to think ahead. Then her gestures will become calm and purposeful and well thought through. She will not run about fetching things, because she has forgotten this or that. Also, to think ahead helps heal the bad manifestations of the will of the child. For example, if a child slams the door, one shouldn't say, "You shouldn't do that." Rather, with full consciousness we should be with the child in the situation in a consequent way. Thus, when the child is approaching the door, we follow the actions in our mind.

The adult also has to be well engaged in work before the children arrive. The mother is already busy when the children awaken in the morning. When the children arrive in the kindergarten in the morning, the adults are already busy there. The will of the child nestles itself into the atmosphere of activity all around, which is created by the adult. The children are totally free to choose their own work. They may be involved in the work of the adults whenever possible.

Another prerequisite for the children's play is that the adults care not only for a rhythmical arrangement of the day, but also for the rhythm of the year in regard to their own working activities. Without being pedantic they can repeatedly do some specific task at certain times. For example, in my kindergarten, in the autumn I am mainly making things for the Christmas bazaar. After Christmas, there is a period when I do embroidery, and after Easter I do wood carving. I do these activities nearly every day for several weeks, and do not do a different activity every day. The one exception is painting day.

Each day, during the free play time, I proceed with my work. I have not created "projects" for the children to do, but I do make certain that enough materials (mostly remnants from my own work) are there for the children to use. All my scraps from cutting fabric or paper, woodcarving or sawing, I put into the children's baskets. The children may freely take what they need from there. They create a variety of things. Some attempt to do what I have done, others have their own ideas. In November, for example, when I glue together the painted and oiled lanterns for the children and then make transparencies for the Christmas bazaar, for at least two weeks every day (except painting day) the big table is set up with scissors, glue and the children's baskets with colored paper. Gold paper pieces are also at hand. Some children make small lanterns and transparencies, others make crowns or other small toys for their dolls, which they then take home with them.

While some children come many days to work at the "glue table," others might not come at all at this time but will come later in the year when I have a time for sewing aprons for the kindergarten or embroidering table covers. Then in the children's baskets there are pretty colored threads for sewing.

Fabric scraps, which are left after cutting, are also placed in the children's baskets for free use.

When I carve small bowls, spoons, candle holders, etc., there are always small pieces of wood left over with which the children build, or which they wax. Carving knives are naturally not put into the children's hands, but sometimes they take pointed sticks and "carve" with them outside on rotting stumps.

In this way the work of the adult is always purposeful and useful for the life of the kindergarten. The children take part in it in a variety of ways, or they play around the teacher who is at work. They are always aware of the work and take a warm and loving interest in it.

In all of this work, there exist the prerequisites of orderliness, rhythm and good habits. They belong to the "right physical environment" in which the children may receive order and strength in their will forces, because they are imitative beings. Imitating is will activity! You cannot teach imitation. It has to be done with one's own will. Will activity is very individual, and it is united with the ego.

We can observe this in the different ways children imitate. Everyone has the same example in front of them in the kindergarten, but their reactions are quite different. Some immediately start to imitate or to play near by, taking in the atmosphere of the working activity, while others don't get the impulse at all. Within imitation there is great freedom. If we are willing to work on ourselves, then we need to also work on the prerequisites described above. Then all the children will find for their will development what they need and what they are unconsciously seeking.

To guide the children in their play we have to always think of the differentiated steps in their development. Now I would like to talk a little more about the last period between five and seven years of age. After age five, a transition takes place from what the child wants to do to what the child should do. This does not mean that we give the children orders or commands that just come into our minds. Rather, out of the strong connection built up with the adults during the preceding years, the children now want to do what they should do. But even though we may use more words and appeal to the mental images of these older kindergarten children, even if we tell them what they can do and how they can do it, even if we inspire their forces of patience, even then: imitation is still the main thing!

Until now the children have unconsciously noticed that the adult has done what was needed in the kindergarten, in order to finish the daily work, to care for the environment, prepare for the festivals, etc. The children have noticed that the adult hasn't always done what she would like to do but rather what she needs to do. This attitude can also be imitated by the children after age five. How? The children observe, for example, that the adult takes a long time for her work. Either she makes many things of the same project such as for festivals or for the bazaar, or she needs a long time to make only one thing such as with carving or embroidery. Children see the perseverance, the

patience and care that the adult brings to her work. They are interested in the process from day to day. They see also that the adult does things that are uncomfortable for her to do, but that she tries to overcome this. For example it may not come naturally to her to sew with a thimble, but she always uses the thimble nevertheless.

Another aid to getting children to do what they should do or how they should do it, is to talk about specific people, how they behave in their profession, what they would do in a certain situation. Between five and seven they do not need to have the physical presence of someone working in front of them; they can also build up a picture inwardly by hearing about the person. For example, I may talk about the master of embroidery who taught me to embroider, or about a tailor who would never sew without a thimble, or about the servant called Ludwig whom I got to know when I went to a conference one day (see "The Story of Ludwig" at the end of this article).

During the second half of the school year before they go into first grade, we may request the oldest children to do a specific task. Then they have the possibility to strengthen their will forces by pursuing a certain goal. I always offer these oldest children the possibility of making their own very simple, knotted dolls. Rudolf Steiner says that a self-made "bajazzo," knotted out of an old rag and with ink spots for eyes, is able to awaken the genius within the child.

We start by embroidering the doll's blanket after Christmas. Then we tease the wool by hand to form the doll's head and knot the hands, using a pink flannel cloth for the doll. The children make their own eye spots using a colored pencil. After that they start sewing the hair and some clothes for the doll. Some children have a great many by the end of the year. Some only one! From the moment the doll is finished, it is integrated into the children's play. One often sees a difference here between boys and girls. The girls feed their dolls and play with them in a variety of ways, and sew them many, many clothes. The boys put them in the cars they build and take them for rides or use them for patients in their ambulances. Over the weekends the children take them home, so that they can be cared for during the weekends as well.

Around age six, the children can also follow instructions. They are asked to do things and they like to do them. For example, they can go as a messenger to another class or get the broom and dustpan, or they may be asked to help dry the dishes. We should never ask for a child's help by questioning the child. Try to know what the specific child is able to do and what the child would like to do, and sometimes what the child needs to do! It may happen that a child rejects doing what you request, but some others then come and ask, "May I do it?"

Children of this age are able to understand our instructions. They can transform the mental image that arises through words into their own activity. In their earlier years we had to divert children from the things that they shouldn't do. Now they need clearly defined limits and clear directions such as "We don't shoot," or "I don't like this." It must be said in such a way that the children still feel the love of the adult and feel the conviction of the adult as a loving and loved authority.

Everything that I have tried to point out here has been said while bearing in mind the words that Rudolf Steiner spoke in a lecture in Dornach on April 19, 1923. (Lecture 5 of *The Child's Changing Consciousness and Waldorf Education*, pg. 110):

"... before the change of teeth [children] live in the region of the will, which ... is intimately connected with the fact that children imitate their surroundings. But what enters the child's being physically at that time also contains moral and spiritual forces, which became firmly established in the child's organism."

This means that the will of the child can be developed and become strong through good habits, consequences, and limits set by the adult as an example.

When the child enters first grade, the will has to be trained more and more consciously. Now children have to follow a task given by the teacher for a period of time, such as watering the flowers, dusting the window sill, or cleaning the blackboard for a week. Children must remember every day and must do it, even if they don't want to. They must learn to overcome themselves. During the kindergarten years it is too early to insist on repeated tasks for particular children. With the most sensitive feeling, we have to guide the children from learning by way of imitation to learning from a loving authority. This is a great art!

I would be glad if what I have said here helps you to appreciate more fully how great the significance of example is for the child's imitation and for the development of the will.

The Story of Ludwig the Servant

Ludwig was a real servant in the home of an elderly lady. We stayed in her home during a weekend conference. At breakfast time when things ran out, Ludwig was there to bring more food.

In the kindergarten I gave a description of Ludwig to the children. After that I asked a six-year-old boy to bring the cups from the tray to everyone's place. He looked over all the cups, chose one out of the middle and put it at his own place, very satisfied for he thought that it was the fullest one. Then he looked at me, by chance, and I said, "Ludwig wouldn't have done that; he always serves the others and takes the last one himself." "Really?" asked the boy. "Really," I answered. Then he took the cup, put it at another place, served all the others and took the last one himself.

Freya Jaffke,
Germany, Waldorf
Kindergarten Association

4. Considerations about Kindergarten Readiness

The needs of modern families are changing dramatically. Yet, the basic needs of the young child are not. According to Drs. Brazelton and Greenspan, in their book *The Irreducible Needs of Children*, the number one need of childhood is for on-going nurturing relationships. A young child continues to need an education that, in the past, transpired in every healthy home. This includes a broad education of the senses, continuity of care, experience in the "Living Arts" realms of domestic, nurturing, and creative experience, as well as the development of social skills.

Yet the demands and stresses on parents increase daily, and the support systems that foster this kind of care of children are vanishing. In the Afterword, Cynthia Aldinger describes the LifeWays approach, which pioneers a new way to offer young children what they have always needed, through the creation of "family suites" where consistent caregivers offer a foundation in all of the above mentioned areas. LifeWays seeks to address the needs not only of children, but the adults who care for them, offering parent education, and caregiver training.

It is an exciting time within the Waldorf Early Childhood Education Movement. Educators are living into the question: what is the proper age for a child to enter a more formal kindergarten setting? Many answers are proliferating. Some Waldorf schools incorporate the three-year-olds into their mixed-age kindergartens. Some offer nursery classes for the threes and young fours. Many schools offer parent-child classes, in which parents and toddlers attend together, under the guidance of an experienced teacher. More schools are now encouraging Waldorf-based home programs that offer small group care. Some schools offer training and support for these home caregivers, and some home care providers seek the LifeWays training. This question will continue to live into our future, and it is in the future that the living answers will unfold.

Although the structure of the educational system may change, given the changing structure of society, the needs of the young child will remain constant. In the following article, we look at some of the hallmarks of "readiness" for entering a more formal kindergarten, in which the class size may be larger, and the demands of stamina and attention span, as well as independence and a more mature social development, are required.

Sharifa Oppenheimer

I N TALKING WITH KINDERGARTEN TEACHERS from all parts of North America, it has become clear that many schools are wrestling with the question of what age children ought to be when they enter our nurseries or kindergartens. Some schools have resolved the question by allowing young threes to enter into a nursery class where they are separate from the fours and fives, while others integrate them into a mixed-age group.

In the book *A Guide to Child Health* (Floris Books), Drs. Michaela Glöckler and Wolfgang Goebel, look at many aspects of the young child's development as well as many types of childhood diseases. We summarize here some of their thoughts on when a child is "ripe" for entering kindergarten:

One milestone is that the child should literally be prepared to take some steps away from the home and mother. The child is ready to enter kindergarten when he wants to stay at a friend's home on his own. As long as the child is still attached to the mother's apron strings, this time of independence has not yet come. In such cases, if the child is over three-and-a-half or four, it may show that the mother's behavior is holding the child back from achieving this important independence.

A second milestone of readiness appears when the child can listen to stories from beginning to end. This shows that the child's ability to visualize or conceptualize (the German word "vorstellen," which lacks a good English translation, is used) can be directly reached through the word. The child is therefore ready to follow directions within a group.

In the experience of these two physicians, these signs are seen at the earliest around age three-and-a-half. If they do not appear by age four, then it may be helpful to speak with the child's pediatrician about this.

Some years ago, when Margret Meyerkort was offering a course at Acorn Hill, we consulted with her about kindergarten readiness. She discussed many of the same considerations offered above by Drs. Jacobi, Glöckler and Göbel, and added a few more. Her list included the following:

1) Today the child often says "I" at the age of two, but the real experience of "I" is later. The "I"-consciousness seems to begin early because the child is brought into thinking earlier than before. We need to discern now between the child's saying "I" and really meaning it, for only when it is truly there is the child able to reach others through speech rather than by hitting;

2) The child needs a certain amount of independence from the parent and should be able to do a certain amount of own dressing and undressing. Needs to be toilet trained and independent of the breast.

3) The child needs to show a certain amount of physiological and psychological stamina. The child should:

   a) be able to stay awake for four hours without needing a nap;

   b) not be so delicate as to catch every little cold in school;

   c) be sufficiently developed to manage childhood diseases and does not get convulsions with high fevers;

   d) be past the first stubborn period of the "terrible twos," which belongs to the period of ego seeking;

   e) have developed the first feeling for time because the ego is there;

   f) be able to take a good walk without stopping for every little stone or puddle.

4) Until two-and-a-half or three the child plays alone. After that, begins to play with others and can imitate activities at the time they are occurring.

5) The child should show the first possibilities of recognizing dangers and thus of not running into the street or pond, and should show the first possibility of self-defense rather than crying. This is an indication that the ego is there to ward off difficulties.

All of the above considerations point to a picture of the child who follows an archetypal pattern of development—speaking around age two and thinking around age three, accompanied by a real statement of "I," also around age three. This is preceded by the difficult stage of the terrible twos when children are creating a distance between themselves and the world around them through the use of "no." It is only after this new "I"-awareness has had time to settle into the child that the child seems ready to reach out to the broader world of the kindergarten.

One can see the stages of development portrayed in the child's drawings. In her book *Understanding Children's Drawings*, Michaela Strauss shows the circular movements drawn by the child under age three. It is around age three that the circular movement develops into a circle with a clear inside and outside (Illustration A). Then she describes the process in this way: "In his drawing the child now tries very hard to make a circle and 'close it', 'join it up'... A little girl is sitting up at the table completely engrossed in drawing circles all over the page. It is her third birthday, and in answer to the question: 'What is your name?' the answer comes pat: 'I? My name is "I!"' This flash of ego-consciousness is documented in the child's drawing by the form of the circle."(A)

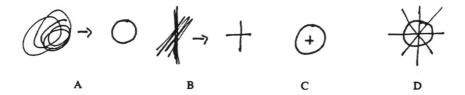

A   B   C   D

Michaela Strauss also describes the more linear form of crayon movement which the one- and two-year-old will also do. By age three this has generally evolved into a clear cross (B). She gives an example of David, who just turned three and preferred drawing with a hard pencil, letting "a mass of lines of the finest filigree arise on the paper, without, however, achieving the cross corresponding to his age. Then the family take David and his younger brother to stay with friends who have five children. They are all older than David. David, the eldest up till now, the 'big' brother, cannot cope at the outset with his new role of 'little one'. So he escapes into illness, has a high temperature and lets himself be spoilt. Three days later he gets up and is well. As though to demonstrate that he can now master the new situation, he takes a thick colored crayon and, for the first time, he draws, one after another, on several sheets of paper, a large perpendicular cross that fills a whole page."

Next the child, after the third year, begins to bring the circle and the cross together and continues to do so in a wide variety of ways "until the fifth year and beyond." The child will put a point or a cross into the middle of the circle, describing a new stage of self-development (C). "He uses these to show his relation to inner and outer space, and he puts a point or a cross in the centre of the inner space to represent himself. In both these symbols he illustrates for the first time his experience of the ego and of the world about him. The point and the cross within a circle represent the 'I-form.'"

Michaela Strauss also gives a picture of the next and perhaps final stage in terms of kindergarten readiness: "Towards the fourth year a new orientation is on its way. The point and the crossing having crystallized as "I"-symbols, this concentration now gradually begins to loosen. The paths of movement lead from inside outwards. To begin with they radiate out from the centre as far as the periphery of the circle and remain within this boundary; this soon becomes more free, however, and groping feelers reach out beyond" (D).

The remarks by Drs. Jacobi, Glöckler and Göbel, as well as Margret Meyerkort and Michaela Strauss all seem to point towards children not being inwardly ready for nursery or mixed-age kindergarten until between three-and-a-half and four. We are then left with the question of why is the trend

developing in American education, including in Waldorf kindergartens, towards bringing the young threes or, in some cases, even two-and-a-half-year-olds into school programs? Perhaps the situation is comparable to why American education has brought academic studies to children age five and younger. On one level the children seem ready. The five-year-old is often asking about how to write, read or do arithmetic. The parent or educator can easily mistake this as a sign of true readiness for the more labored instruction that goes on in teaching academics, whereas in my experience most five-year-olds are content to learn to write and read a few words, just enough to feel "grown up." Now they can announce that they can read or write, just as they announce to their parents that they can speak German after they have done one or two verses in that language in the kindergarten. In other words, a little bit goes a long way.

With the two-year-old who is precociously saying "I" the same may be true. Parents and educators may be easily mistaking this as a true ego-conscious experience and begin creating an educational experience for the child that is not yet appropriate. Even when the "I" is more fully established at age three, the above indications point to the child needing another six to twelve months in order to be inwardly ready to take steps out into the world.

What then are the possibilities for the child before the age of three-and-a-half or four? Many children stay at home with their mothers until this age with perhaps a morning or two a week when mother and child may visit another family or host a family. This puts little strain on the child who, at the same time, has a social experience with another child of the same age. There are also many families where the mother needs to work, or feels she cannot be at home so much with her young child, or feels the child is especially hungry for social contact. Some of the alternatives being explored in Waldorf settings for younger children are home-based play groups or day care centers, ranging in size from three or four children to six or eight. We have also heard of some play groups where the mothers are present with the young children, making toys while the children play, and learning songs, verses and stories along with their children. In such a program mothers can also receive much help with their basic questions about parenting a young child.

As Waldorf educators in North America we are just beginning to explore these questions of kindergarten readiness, and we recognize a certain urgency as more and more mothers of children under three are going back to work or are seeking a nursery program for children.

Joan Almon,
USA, Alliance for Childhood

Afterword

Meeting the Needs of the Times

Cynthia K. Aldinger

LifeWays North America

This afterword offers a brief overview of the expansion of the Waldorf/Steiner Early Childhood Movement in North America from being primarily a kindergarten movement to the inclusion of parent-child programs, extended day programs and child care. It introduces the work of LifeWays North America as representing one model of care that has developed from the Waldorf/Steiner Early Childhood Movement.

Rudolf Steiner believed that one of the essential aspects of education was to teach in such a way that the children would learn how to properly breathe. In early childhood we might say "to live in such a way that the children will learn how to breathe."

As a young child in the 1950s, when my mother worked part-time I was always with my grandparents. On days my mother did not work, I was home —all day—several days in a row. Occasionally, mother would go to a neighbor's home for coffee and a chat, and I would go with her and play with the children of that household. Whether I was at grandma's house or at home, I was playing by myself or with neighborhood children while the adults went about tending the home. Often my mother would gather the neighborhood children together and sing with us and read stories. It was not called "home-based preschool" back then. It was just life, like breathing.

Thirty years later, when I was teaching in a mixed-age Waldorf kindergarten, it was a joy to create the flow of activities, time for active robust play and for quiet listening, for being together in a group or skipping away with a best friend, for cleaning and caring, for baking and eating, time to create useful and beautiful things and time to dig in the sand. The daily, weekly and seasonal rhythms were like breathing in and out.

The Waldorf kindergarten was, and is, a place that honors childhood. In my experience, it was even more. It was a haven. As a founding teacher, there was always more to deal with than just the parents and children of my own kindergarten. There were faculty meetings, college meetings, board meetings, festival committee meetings, long-range planning meetings, and so on. Going out into the school to attend to such things was like venturing out into the world. Returning to my kindergarten was like "coming home." Elementary school colleagues would occasionally come into my kindergarten in the afternoon to rest while their children were with another teacher. The couch was there to welcome them.

The kindergarten was not a classroom. It was a child's play garden. Over the years as the kindergarten became more and more permeated with our routines and rituals, our ebbs and flows, our happys and sads, our work and play, the room became like a silent pedagogue, the walls embracing us like a benevolent grandmother who sees all but knows when to turn her head to allow just the right measure of mischief. I remember those joyful occasions when I would step out of the room just before clean up time was finished, knowing the pure delight it provided the children to "barricade" the door while they completed the final details of putting things away. When the children opened the door, I would walk back in, not as the teacher, but as the village inspector to a chorus of giggles as I noticed all the marvelous detail that had gone into the tidying away. We were our own little community, and even when I was a younger teacher, I felt like the beloved grandmother or auntie who welcomed the neighborhood children over to play for a few hours in the morning. At the end of the morning, the children left with their parents or caregivers to go home or to visit with friends.

Over the years some things began to change. Children who had been in traditional institutional child care since infancy were beginning to come into the kindergarten. Many of them did not understand how to enter into self-directed imaginative play. Other children came who had not been in child care but had been enrolled in multiple enrichment programs since toddlerhood. Many children also needed care beyond the kindergarten morning. Some families requested this extension because both parents needed to work in order to afford tuition for a Waldorf/Steiner School. Others simply felt that their children thrived in the longer day at the kindergarten with other children rather than at home. The reasons for wanting the longer hours varied, but the requests were strong. Also, more families with children younger than three emphatically asked, "What programs do you have for my child?" They made it clear that, while Waldorf/Steiner education was their first choice, if our schools could not serve their needs, they would go elsewhere.

Parents were seeking "more" for their children—more hours, more years in school, more activities, more time away from home. In this age of individualized loneliness, parents were also seeking community and were asking for guidance on how to be with their children.

How were we, as Waldorf schools, going to meet these needs?

Schools began offering extended days. Children who needed the extended day would gather from all of the early childhood programs and have lunch together, followed by rest time, then a light snack and a bit more play time before being picked up. Some schools included lunch as part of the kindergartens and then dismissed the children to After Care or to go home. Typically the early childhood After Care program ended when the elementary school day ended around 3:00 p.m. Children who needed even later care would go to another After Care program until 5 or 6 p.m. This continues to be the pattern for many schools. Others are beginning to offer full-day kindergartens to avoid so much switching around for the children.

To respond to parents' requests to serve younger children, many schools began offering "nursery" or "pre-school" programs for children just under three to a little over four. Some even began accepting a few two-year-olds. At my school it was called the Wonder Garden, and I remember the wise insights of its first teacher Laura Cassidy when she noted that it simply did not work to have a "pressed down" kindergarten morning for these little ones. She noted how much slower the pace needed to be with only little ones present and no older children there to help or model for them. She recognized that bodily care, dressing and undressing, toileting, and such were valid and important parts of their daily experience and needed to be given plenty of time.

Schools also began offering programs to stem the tide of loneliness of the parents and to bring in even younger children. Called parent-child programs or playgroups, these programs were usually one morning a week for a couple of hours. In some schools, parent-infant or parent-toddler programs were also offered. They have become so popular that several groups convene throughout the week. Many schools have begun to see them as enrollment builders, although many teachers view them primarily as support for parents. They want to strengthen the healthy development of families regardless of whether the families later enroll in their schools. Typically, many families do enroll in the school because they have been inspired by their experience in the parent-child programs.

These expanding programs that kept the children at the school longer hours and brought children out of their homes at younger and younger ages were not entirely welcomed into the Waldorf/Steiner Early Childhood Movement. In some schools, yes, there was excitement about this development. In others it was regarded with some trepidation. Still others chose not to have young children in any school program other than the kindergartens. Why the resistance?

Dr. Steiner speaks of the first three years of life with great reverence. He impels us to understand the depth of responsibility we take on when in the presence of these little ones so recently arrived from the realms of spirit.

The first two-and-a-half years are the most important of all. During this time children have the gift of being instinctively aware of everything that goes on around them, especially as regards the people who come in daily contact with them. Everything that takes place in their environment imprints itself on their physical bodily form ... so that our behavior will influence their disposition to health or disease for the whole of life.[1]

As the poet William Wordsworth wrote in his poem "Ode to Immortality," "trailing clouds of glory do we come from God who is our home." The Waldorf Movement has a very protective gesture toward this early period of life, holding as an ideal the image of the child at home, cared for by a loving family. To open programs for children under three-and-a-half, even though accompanied by their parents, is a big step to take.

Yet the phenomenon of playgroups is becoming a cultural norm. If we do not provide these opportunities, parents will find them elsewhere. Many schools decided it would be wise to support families who were seeking not only community with other parents but also guidance about raising their children. Today parent-child teachers are grateful to meet these families who, regardless of lifestyle and parenting practices, have found their way to Waldorf schools. Every parent-child teacher can share testimonials of how the program has helped families make life-changing choices for their homes.

Considering the resistance to extending the school day for kindergarten children, again, there was a long-held belief that the best place for young children was the home. The hope was that after a morning in the kindergarten, the children would go home and have lunch followed by a nap, then an afternoon of play. What has been happening for years, however, in North America, is that children who were being picked up after kindergarten were not necessarily going home. Perhaps they were going out to lunch and then to run errands or to attend a variety of "enrichment" classes such as ballet, music, gymnastics, or sports. Partly for this reason, some schools began adding lunch to the end of the kindergarten morning. Others began experimenting with extended day programs.

1 *Understanding Young Children,* extracts from lectures by Rudolf Steiner. International Association of Waldorf Kindergartens, 1975.

At my school our first attempt at offering an extended day for the kindergarten children resulted in cranky, tired children coming to school the next day after they attended After Care. Over the years and with dedicated intention on the part of those carrying the afternoon program, things improved. We changed the name from After Care to TLC (Tender Loving Care) and consciousness was given to how the transition took place from the kindergarten morning to the afternoon. The kindergarten teachers worked with the TLC teachers to build a conscious bridge of care and loving exchange. Currently most schools offer some type of extended day for their early childhood children.

Today a common experience in Waldorf schools is as follows: a child as young as an infant or toddler comes to school with a parent or caregiver to attend a parent-child program for a few years, followed by attending a nursery or pre-school program for a year or two, followed by attending a kindergarten program, and often spending the afternoons with different teachers in an extended day program. Some children experience two extended day programs because the program for young children ends at 3:00 or so, and then they switch to the "after school" program that goes to 5:00 or 6:00 p.m. In the course of a day, they may have been with three different sets of teachers. The good news is that the children do not have to travel to a whole different school or day care program in the afternoons.

However, for many Steiner/Waldorf early childhood educators this is not the type of schedule they consider ideal for young children. In *The Child's Changing Consciousness* Steiner said: "The task of the kindergarten teacher is to adapt the practical activities of daily life so that they are suitable for the child's imitation through play… The activities of children in kindergarten must be derived directly from life itself rather than being 'thought out' by the intellectualized culture of adults. In the kindergarten, the most important thing is to give the children the opportunity to directly imitate life itself."

Taking into account the current culture of adult life in the Western world with its busyness and days filled with a variety of activities and comings and goings and restlessness, this model of shifting the children from one setting to the next throughout the day is very contemporary. But is it the lifestyle we want them to imitate when they are so young? Does it allow the space and time for them to penetrate their play? Does it meet the fundamental needs of the young child?

"The joy of children in and with their environment must therefore be counted among the forces that build and shape the physical organs."(Rudolf

Steiner, *The Kingdom of Childhood*) Compare what Steiner said in *Essentials of Education*: "For the small child before the change of teeth, the most important thing in education is the teacher's own being" to what contemporary pediatrician Dr. T. Berry Brazelton says in his book *The Irreducible Needs of Children*: "Supportive, warm, nurturing emotional interactions with infants and young children ... help the central nervous system grow appropriately." While young children may exhibit amazing levels of resiliency, are we best serving their needs by shifting their environment and their teachers/caregivers so frequently?

In the mid-nineties, the Waldorf Kindergarten Association noticed that many teachers had begun caring for children in their homes, some for personal reasons and others because they felt that they could better provide the type of seamless day and rhythmical flow in which young children thrive. At the East Coast Waldorf Kindergarten Conference in 1996 one of the workshops was specifically for individuals offering child care in homes or centers. Many who attended spoke with tender vulnerability of their sense of being viewed as "wrong" to offer care for infants and toddlers or to offer care for longer days. They experienced a pervasive feeling that this was not the Waldorf way and that children needed to be at home before the kindergarten years and needed to go back home each day after kindergarten.

Rather than being criticized for their efforts, the people attending the workshop were thanked for taking the courageous step of trying to meet the needs of the times. Not long after that, the Waldorf Kindergarten Association changed its name to the Waldorf Early Childhood Association of North America (WECAN), sending a clear message that they were not only an association of teachers in kindergartens but also included colleagues in a variety of other venues.

Around this same time, Rena Osmer and I, both WECAN board members, began traveling and visiting traditional child care centers in the U.S. and studying the changes that were taking place in homelife. There had been a paradigm shift regarding the daily life of the young child. Typically fifty years ago, the home was the place where the children played and hung out and learned about daily life, and the kindergarten was where parents sent them for artistic and playful enrichment for a couple of hours in the morning. The parental home was still the place where children experienced the main thrust of domestic life. Currently in our culture, parents are drawn to taking their children out of the home for increased stimuli. The activities of "housekeeping" or "homemaking" are sometimes relegated to being done when the children are not at home or when they are sleeping. As will be mentioned later, the daily life experiences of what makes a household function are becoming less and less common for children.

Rena and I became convinced that it was time for Steiner-based child care and support for parents to grow and be strengthened in North America. With respect toward those who had already begun to work in these arenas and with an interest in expanding even further, we explored the question of what we thought Steiner-based child care would ideally look like. Our conclusion was that it would be imitative of the qualities and activities found in healthy, rhythmical home life — the ways of life. Thus came the name Life-Ways which we adapted from our friends who wrote the first Lifeways books. By 1998, the first LifeWays Child Care Center was opened in rural southeast Wisconsin, and several others have opened since.

LifeWays centers and homes are designed to feel like home-away-from-home. Too often the missing ingredients in traditional child care settings are consistency, warmth, and long lasting relationships. The heart of LifeWays childcare is the "Family Suite" in which children, caregivers, and families develop long term relationships in an environment that protects childhood and enhances optimal physical, socio-emotional, cognitive and spiritual health for the children and the caregivers. What ages the various sites care for and how long their days run vary from place to place.

The Milwaukee LifeWays Child Development Center has three suites with a full blend of ages from infant to six. They offer care from 7:30 a.m. to 5:30 p.m. Some caregivers choose to work for eight hours a day while others prefer to share a suite and work part-time. Set up to imitate a large family, there are usually seven to eight children in a suite with a primary caregiver. With three suites, they function like a small neighborhood or extended family. All the children get to know all the caregivers, and they have a special connection to their primary caregivers. The caregivers are supported by a part-time administrator (who is also the parent-child teacher), other part-time caregivers, a cook, a kindergarten teacher, and volunteers. The older children of the suites may attend the preschool or the forest kindergarten two or three mornings a week and are sometimes joined by community children who come only for the preschool or kindergarten. During this time, the youngest children in the suites have a quiet time with their caregivers, similar to how it is at home when older siblings go off to school for awhile. When they return to the suite, the infants and toddlers are delighted to see them.

In addition to LifeWays centers, there are individuals who offer LifeWays child care and/or preschool in their homes. In many ways this is ideal because they are already in a home so they don't have to imitate being in a home. Trisha Lambert in Davis, California, is a "Full" WECAN member and a LifeWays "Representative." She was a Waldorf Kindergarten teacher in a school before deciding to offer care at her home. She was doing this already before the LifeWays organization began. Initially inspired by Helle Heckman in Denmark, Trisha and the children spend a long time outside each day exploring the numerous gardens and grounds surrounding her home. Trisha prepares meals and snacks for the children, and they sleep in the living room and bedroom of her home. Most days they have a little time for some simple circle games and a story, and if there is a baby in the mix, the baby plays or sleeps while the other children sing and play. Like the Milwaukee LifeWays Center, Trisha has an ongoing waiting list. Many families can feel that the simplicity of daily living offered in these settings is what best serves their children, and often wonderful stories emerge of how families begin to slowly transform their own homes to be more reflective of the practices they have observed.

The rhythms and activities of the days and weeks in a LifeWays setting are meant to imitate home life rather than school life—daily care and cleaning of the environment, bodily care of the children, doing laundry, putting away groceries, eating, sleeping, singing and playing, crafting for special seasonal activities. While the cook prepares the organic lunch each day, the caregivers and children in each suite participate throughout the week in the preparation of the food—for example, peeling carrots, chopping onions, etc. Whether or not the children actively participate in the work being done, they thrive within the environment of the focused work of their caregivers.

Called "The Living Arts" (Domestic, Nurturing, Creative and Social), these daily life activities are quietly disappearing from the routine experience of many children today. In full-day care it is easier to experience a natural flow of these activities without feeling hurried. One notices that the children have more time to penetrate such things as putting on their shoes, brushing their teeth, having their hair brushed, getting dressed to go outside, watching a baby being fed or diapered. The breath of the mid-day sleep also helps. Whether or not the caregiver also sleeps (some do), there is a natural shift that takes place that allows for a qualitatively different experience from morning to afternoon. When they awaken from nap and have their hair brushed and faces oiled (a practice adopted from Bernadette Raichle's Awhina Child Care Center in New Zealand), they are ready for the slower pace of afternoon play and getting ready to go home.

The caregivers attend a mentor-supported one-year part-time LifeWays training that introduces them to the Living Arts as well as to the LifeWays principles and suggested practices. Human development is taught from the spiritual scientific insights of Rudolf Steiner and contemporary child development experts. Students experience music, movement and speech classes to strengthen them as human beings worthy of being imitated by young children and are offered numerous handwork classes, including an introduction to gardening, to steep them in the practical, yet aesthetic, craft of homemaking. Other parts of the training focus on working with regulatory agencies as well as how to work with parents and colleagues. A unique aspect of the LifeWays training is that the students are comprised of parents, child care providers, home-based preschool teachers, parent educators and grandparents. The common denominator is the understanding that the fundamental needs of young children can be met through the life activity of the home regardless of whether you are a stay-at-home parent or a child care provider or a parent educator.

Just as it was a privilege to teach in a Waldorf kindergarten so many years ago, it is an equal privilege to be a part of the ongoing development of Steiner-inspired child care. While going back in time is not the answer, many Waldorf/Steiner early childhood educators have discovered the value of slowing down, shifting the emphasis to daily life activities, and expanding their time with children in their care. LifeWays is one part of this expanded work of Waldorf/Steiner educators. There are others who have been offering child care for two decades or longer, and there are others offering training and support for parent-child teachers and teachers who wish to be involved with birth-to-three work.

At the Waldorf Early Childhood Conference in New York in 2006, the keynote speaker was Dr. Michaela Glöckler, director of the medical section at the Goetheanum. Susan Silverio, director of the Northeast LifeWays training, shared her notes quoting Dr. Glöckler as follows: "Teach beyond guilt. Teach out of Joy! Open up kindergartens outside of the school landscape! Organize farming/play afternoons in family homes. Receive children as early as possible and keep them as long as possible."

We are pleased to be involved with this expanded consciousness around early childhood practices and family support, and we are grateful to the Waldorf Early Childhood Association of North America for having the foresight and warmth of heart to support individuals and organizations that are furthering the work. It is a breath of fresh air.